Vanishing Country Houses
of Ireland

First published in 1988 by
The Irish Architectural Archive and
The Irish Georgian Society.

Second Edition 1989

Designed by Ted and Ursula O'Brien, Oben Design.
Phototypeset by Oben in *Baskerville II* on Compugraphic® MCS8200.
Reproduction of duo-tone photographs by Colour Repro Ltd., Dublin.

Printed by W. & G. Baird Ltd., Antrim on 135gsm art paper.

ISBN 0 948018 08 9   Cased
ISBN 0 948018 09 7   Paperback

Vanishing Country Houses of Ireland

The Knight of Glin
David J. Griffin
Nicholas K. Robinson

Published by
The Irish Architectural Archive and The Irish Georgian Society

with sponsorship for this edition from
Christie Manson & Woods

The authors and publishers would like to thank
Christie Manson & Woods,
without whose generous sponsorship
publication of this second edition
would not have been possible.

LIST OF CONTENTS

Acknowledgements

This book, first published in December 1988, in the 25th year of the Irish Georgian Society, marks a long-standing collaboration between the Society and the Irish Architectural Archive. It spotlights a problem – of decay, loss and destruction: here are the broken columns, the shattered pinnacles, the collapsed ceilings which were fashioned by generations of nameless Irish artists and craftsmen. Myths die hard, and you will still be told that many a plaster ceiling was the work of Italians, or foreigners. This is rarely true. The buildings of Ireland are – overwhelmingly – the work of native craftsmen.

Or were. Various responses have been made to the destruction which is recorded here. Reports have appeared* chronicling the madness of not exploiting (even in terms of the tourist industry) the resources of these buildings. Nick Robinson in his essay indicates the responses of an attentive if not always encouraging government. The IGS's response was to roll up its sleeves and get on with the backbreaking job of actually saving and repairing the buildings. The response of the IAA was to collect photographs, drawings, models and all other kinds of record so that the full story of these buildings could be told. One of its earliest purchases was the IGS collection of photographs which formed the nucleus of what is now on display. Houses in Northern Ireland have not been included since the various arrangements for conservation, preservation and restoration prevailing there are quite different from those in the Republic.

The authors are grateful to many for help in the preparation of this sad record and its accompanying exhibition. First among these is Mark Bence-Jones, whose *Guide to Irish Country Houses* is a magisterial record of the surviving as well as the vanished country houses of the whole island. The unpublished lists compiled by Maurice Craig and William Garner for An Foras Forbartha have also been of great use. Special thanks are due to Edwin Davison and Sean O'Reilly who mounted the exhibition. The whole project would not have been possible without the generous financial support of Christie's and the Rohan Group who sponsored the first edition and exhibition and we are particularly grateful to Noel Annesley and Ken Rohan for all their help. This edition has received further sponsorship from Christie's and we are also indebted to our printers, W. & G. Baird, for their support and encouragement as well as for their professional skill.

We would also like to especially thank the following: Daniel Gillman for permission to copy and use photographs from his unique collection and for much help, advice and hospitality on our numerous visits to his home; David Davison who so expertly copied and printed most of the photographs in this book; Ted and Ursula O'Brien, our designers, whose contribution has been enormous; Donal Ó Lunaigh, National Library of Ireland, for permission to use photographs from the Lawrence Collection; Jane Fenlon for typing the manuscript; Frederick O'Dwyer; Ian Lumley; Edward McParland; Peter Pearson; Rose Dunne; Ann Simmons; Kevin B. Nolan; John Harris; Hugh and Grania Weir; Larry Walsh; Edna Longley; Harry McDowell; Eamon Conway; Thomas Pakenham; Andrew Robinson.

May 1989.

The Knight of Glin
David J. Griffin
Nicholas K. Robinson.

* *Heritage at Risk* (1977), *Safeguarding Historic Houses* (1985).

PREFACE

Noel Grove Annesley,
Deputy Chairman,
Christie, Manson & Woods.

As an Irishman I am particularly pleased that Christie's, together with the Rohan group, are supporting the publication of this book and the exhibitions that accompany its appearance. James Christie founded the firm that bears his name in 1766 and it was by a coincidence which gives me pleasure that the same year my forebear Robert, 1st Earl Annesley, married Mary Grove and brought into the family the property in north Cork, subsequently rechristened Annes Grove, where my brother Patrick lives now and welcomes thousands of visitors to the gardens each year.

Many of the photographs in this book, whether interiors or exteriors of houses, give suggestive glimpses of gardens that embellished them, and now these, too, never so numerous, have largely disappeared. Gardens, even more than houses, can give different pleasures at different seasons of the year and it is a theme of this book that Ireland can ill afford to neglect its tourist attractions. Families like ours who have been fortunate enough to inherit old properties, naturally hope that they will be able to hand on these to be maintained by their own successors for the general good, but the political and economic situation since World War II has meant that many owners of old houses, and their collections, great and small, whose English counterparts have been able to think in more constructive terms, have been left no alternative but to sell up.

Of the many Irish houses where sales have been conducted, only in two instances, Malahide and Newbridge, has official intervention ensured the survival of even a proportion of the collection in its intended home. It is much to be hoped that the arrangement whereby Newbridge has been acquired by Dublin County Council, the greater proportion of the Cobbe family collection remains *in situ* and the family continues in residence, is a heartening portent for the future.

No one who loves Ireland can fail to be saddened by the passing of its houses. The Knight of Glin's introduction and the photographs will summon up a host of personal memories. Bowen's Court, for instance, made an impression on me as the scene for the children's parties that I most enjoyed. Elizabeth Bowen, devoted to children though childless herself, organised extraordinary games of pelmanism and we were free to roam across the attic floor open under the whole span of the roof. Byblox, another neighbouring house in north Cork, boxy Georgian, as the name might imply, was another favourite. Both have completely disappeared: the thought is still shocking after many years.

Yet it should be emphasised that the importance of many Irish houses far transcends the human context; too many Irishmen forget that our country's greatest contribution to eighteenth-century civilisation, made by builder and craftsman alike, was in the sphere of architecture.

For Irish Palladianism, like that of America, is as distinct from the architecture of the Whig ascendancy in England as is the latter from the Italian sources from which it drew its inspiration. Irishmen from all over the world have come to take part in the celebrations of Dublin's millennium. It seems sadly appropriate that the Dublin exhibition should be held in a city where so many handsome buildings have disappeared in living memory. Nostalgia may preserve the memory of so precious an artistic patrimony; only official awareness and vigorous support can, at this late stage, preserve what yet remains of this, a unique inheritance, in which everyone of Irish extraction should take pride.

FOREWORD

Kevin B. Nowlan, Chairman,
Joint Working Party on Historic Properties,
and
Pyers O'Conor-Nash, Chairman,
Historic Irish Tourist Houses & Gardens Association (HITHA).

We welcome the decision to reprint *Vanishing Country Houses of Ireland*. The sustained demand for the first printing of the book and the strong expressions of concern which its message evoked, in the world press and on television and radio, are measures of a new awareness about the loss of so much of an architectural heritage which belongs to western society as a whole.

A wide popular appreciation of the cultural and recreational value of heritage properties is now an established international trend and a welcome one. In Ireland, it is important that the policy-makers come to appreciate fully the substantial contribution which a sound policy of architectural conservation can make to the cultural and economic life of the nation. The country houses, with their gardens, and the fine though diminishing stock of vernacular buildings, if loved and respected, can not only help the national tourist industry but also stimulate employment in the local communities for skills old and new.

Recent tax concessions have contributed to an easing of the financial pressures on the owners of heritage properties, provided they have the necessary income to benefit from such concessions, but major financial and administrative problems still remain. Representing the principal environmental bodies in Ireland, we believe that a position has been reached where, in the absence of an adequately endowed organisation capable of protecting our heritage properties, the future is, indeed, bleak for a great legacy of architecture.

We consider that a national property-owning trust, in association with the National Heritage Council, recently established by the Government, could work effectively to avert the loss of a great inheritance. Such a property-owning trust would need financial aid from many sources, not least from the State and the European Community, but the rewards would be great. Without a structured approach and the will to resolve the problem, little will be achieved.

There are, however, some encouraging signs. The setting up of the National Heritage Council is one and Bord Fáilte, the Irish Tourist Board, in its new programme, 'Development for Growth', lays special emphasis on the role of the great houses and historical townscapes in its plans for Irish tourism. This policy is reinforced, too, by the production of attractive tourist information on historic houses and gardens and by the successful cooperation between tourist bodies and local authorities which has resulted in the splendid restoration of Newbridge House and the safeguarding of Malahide Castle, both in Co. Dublin. Again, two houses listed in *Vanishing Country Houses* as 'Derelict' are being restored by private initiative (Markree Castle, Co. Sligo and Gaulstown, Co. Westmeath). Much can be done, but the time for action is fast running out.

THE IRISH GEORGIAN SOCIETY

Desmond Guinness
President, Irish Georgian Society

The Irish Georgian Society was formed in 1958 to work for the preservation of Ireland's architectural heritage, with particular reference to the Georgian period. It carries out rescue and repair work and has helped to save many buildings that were abandoned to the mercy of wind and weather, such as Tailor's Hall and St. Catherine's Church in Dublin. Three Georgian houses on the north side of the Liffey are at present being restored with the help of the Society. Its main achievement has been the saving of Castletown, the magnificent Palladian house in Co. Kildare, which for sixteen years served as the Society's headquarters and to which members enjoy free access. Castletown became the first house open to the public in the Dublin area; the Historic Irish Tourist Houses and Gardens Association (HITHA) was born here, as was the Festival of Music in Great Irish Houses which takes place in June each year. It is now owned and run by an independent body, the Castletown Foundation. The Damer House in Co. Tipperary and Roundwood, Co. Leix, were rescued, restored and passed on to others to use and maintain.

Doneraile Court, Co. Cork, abandoned for seven years by the State, is being gradually restored by the Society and will be opened to the public in due course in conjunction with the Wild Life Park. When Riverstown House, Co. Cork, was restored by the Society and opened to the public in 1966, it was only the third house in the Republic to open its doors to visitors on a regular basis. The Society has always believed that State involvement in the saving of the Irish heritage will only come about through tourism.

Funds are raised by Chapters in the U.K. and the U.S.A. as well as in Ireland and the Samuel H. Kress Foundation has been a most generous contributor. The Society works with Aer Lingus on a scheme for U.S. museum memberships to visit Ireland to see the art and architecture of the Georgian era, and a per capita donation is incorporated in the cost of the tour. The Scalamandré fabric and wallpaper company of New York and the Kindel furniture company of Michigan have both developed an Irish Georgian line and a percentage of their sales helps further the Society's restoration work in Ireland.

In the unfortunate absence of an Historic Buildings Fund in the Republic, grants are given to privately owned houses – Ledwithstown, Glencullen, Freame Mount, etc. Rescue operations have been carried out on numerous follies, gateways, columns, temples, funereal monuments and chapels which do not demand subsequent maintenance. Current rescue operations include the O'Callaghan Mausoleum in Shanrahan graveyard, Co. Tipperary, which houses a grandiose monument carved by David Sheehan in 1742.

An example of our work was the finding of a new home for the Browne's Hill entrance gates, now at Lyons, Co. Kildare, when they were threatened with the bulldozer by the Land Commission. We have also helped a young couple to buy a house in Henrietta Street, Dublin, and in finding and installing a staircase there where the original had been ripped out in order to fit in more tenants.

A Newsletter describing the work of the Society is sent to the membership and a Bulletin is published with articles on Irish art and architecture; back numbers are available. Contributors have included Molly Keane, John Betjeman, Mark Bence-Jones, Maurice Craig, The Knight of Glin, Anne Crookshank, Alistair Rowan, John Harris, C.P. Curran, James White, Ada Leask, Edward McParland, J.H. Andrews, Constantine Fitzgibbon and David S. Howard. A list of books on Irish art and architecture will be sent on request. Copies of rare Irish maps, as well as table mats based on the art of Samuel Dixon, Robert Healy and J.P. Neale, are manufactured and sold for the benefit of the Society; a catalogue of our goods is available.

New members are needed. Apply to: The Irish Georgian Society, Leixlip Castle, Leixlip, Co. Kildare, Ireland. Tel: Dublin (01) 244211.

WASTING ASSETS

Nicholas K Robinson

'The admirers of Ruins need not take the long and hazardous Journeys to Balbeck and Palmyra: a reasonable curiosity may be satisfied by travelling round this Kingdom in that respect.'[1]

o wrote Chief Baron Willes as he journeyed around Ireland in the 1750's. Over two hundred years later Mark Bence-Jones wrote

'Encouraging the belief that almost every Irish country house was "burnt in the Troubles", the ruined country house is an all-too-frequent sight in Ireland . . . In fact, the great majority of these ruined houses were not burnt but either dismantled or allowed to fall down.'[2]

Few would actively rejoice nowadays at this state of affairs. Ruins may be picturesque, or they may look romantic from a distance. The cleared site of a great demolished building might support a crop, or accommodate a car-park. But there is a growing awareness that such scenic or economic advantages may represent a poor return on what – differently treated – could turn out to be a national asset. The Royal Hospital Kilmainham could make a great ruin; so could the Tower of London, or Versailles. But the English and the French, indeed the universal, experience no less than our own is that the proper management of such resources involves the conservation of these great buildings and their appropriate use, often as busy tourist centres. Among all the other good reasons for general satisfaction that Malahide Castle, or Newbridge House have been saved is that they make such a useful contribution to the tourist attractiveness of County Dublin and thus to the economy. The tourist industry could ill afford to lose Westport House and Bantry House and Bunratty Castle and Russborough and their like.

In 1986, properties in the Republic of Ireland affiliated to the Historic Irish Tourist Houses and Gardens Association were visited by over one and a half million people. In the same year 30% of all holiday makers (42% of North American visitors) visited historic houses and gardens, while a mere 15% engaged in fishing, and 8% in golf. As ruins, or as cleared sites, lost country houses would be so many wasted national assets. It is accepted that we should not poison our lakes. We don't plough up our golf courses. The case should be equally obvious that we cannot let our country houses disappear.

But still they are under threat; the story told in these tragic photographs, of misadventure and squandered opportunities, is not finished. How will it end?

There are hopeful signs. An Taisce – the National Trust for Ireland[3] published *Heritage at Risk*[4] in 1977, a seminal report on the future of historic houses, gardens and collections in the Republic of Ireland. Successive governments have responded to its recommendations: tax concessions to owners of heritage properties were announced in the 1978 budget, legislation in subsequent Finance Acts offset the cost of repairs for houses of cultural and historical value against tax liabilities and afforded relief from capital taxes in cases where the public had a reasonable access to such properties. Not all owners or custodians, however, are in a position to benefit from tax relief and the deteriorating situation of heritage properties led to the establishment in 1982 of the Irish Historic Properties Committee. This body, independent of any other conservation group, set itself the task of examining possible structures for a new property-owning trust, broadly on the lines of the National Trust in Britain. It published its report, *Safeguarding Historic Houses*[5], in 1985 recommending the establishment of an independent property-owning trust as a charitable company, with a commitment to heritage properties of all types, to the development of tourism, and to the strengthening of the national economy. It recommended further the setting up of a Heritage Commission to be appointed by the Taoiseach, to administer funds provided by the state for the purpose of supporting historic properties by means of grant or loan. A joint working party[6] has recently urged the government to create a national property-owning trust to undertake the separate tasks of custody, operation and funding of key buildings, gardens, parklands and collections (including vernacular properties) not in state care.

Meanwhile, government was tackling the business of setting up a heritage commission. The Heritage Advisory Committee was appointed by the outgoing Taoiseach, Dr. Garret FitzGerald, in 1987 to advise government on the conservation of Ireland's architectural heritage and the disbursement of funds from the national lottery towards the maintenance and repair of privately held historic buildings.

This body was not proceeded with by the present Taoiseach, Mr Charles Haughey, when he assumed office in 1987. He decided to create, instead, a broader based National Heritage Council to cover archaeology, wildlife, landscape, heritage gardens and inland waterways as well. It is hoped that the Council, established in August 1988 under the chairmanship of Lord Killanin, will develop a vigorous policy for architectural conservation and will win financial support for its implementation. It should be noted that it was Mr. Haughey, then Minister for Finance, who commissioned An Taisce in 1969 to make an inventory of Ireland's outstanding country houses and gardens.

The picture, then, is one of intense activity on the part of voluntary bodies concerned with the survival of historic buildings as cultural and economic assets; activity which is attended to by government unevenly, understandable in a time of unusual stringency of public spending. While recommendations for a system of grants to private owners of historic buildings have – up to the time of writing – been ineffectual, concessions within the area of capital acquisitions tax, capital gains tax and income tax have been of profound significance.

But the problems so starkly presented in the pages which follow can be tackled comprehensively only by the setting up of a non-governmental property-owning trust. Similar bodies have long existed in other countries and have benefited by the existence of private wealth, unparalleled in Ireland, in putting together major portfolios of endowed properties. Northern Ireland has been fortunate in that the National Trust administers properties there as well as in Britain. We in the Republic are almost, but not quite, too late into the field and have to tackle the additional problem that in many cases owners are quite simply not in a position to endow properties which they might be prepared to hand over to a National Trust.

In discussing the tragedy of the wasting assets of Ireland's vanishing country houses, I have endeavoured to strike a note of optimism. The intensity of discussion, directed at an attentive, if not always responsive, government comes at a time when a solution is still possible. Individual trusts (such as the Alfred Beit Foundation which owns Russborough, the Castletown Foundation which owns Castletown, the Irish Georgian Foundation which leases Doneraile Court, and the Birr Scientific Heritage Foundation which owns the great scientific collections at Birr Castle) have set precedents, albeit sporadic and unco-ordinated, in the non-governmental area. In addition, individual arrangements, also unco-ordinated, have been entered into with the state (as at Mount Congreve, Co. Waterford and Glenveigh Castle, Co. Donegal) or with local authorities and tourist bodies (as at Malahide Castle, Newbridge, both in Co. Dublin, Robertstown, Co. Kildare and Belvedere, Co. Westmeath) to ensure the survival of important properties.

The Irish Georgian Society has an unparalleled record over its thirty years of existence of saving and restoring houses such as Castletown, Damer House Roscrea, and Roundwood near Mountrath. The mood and the fashions of the 1980's are conservationist and there now is, in Ireland, what until recently has been seriously lacking, an academic basis for the preservation and planning of the architectural heritage, namely the Irish Architectural Archive.

In 1976 Ireland was the only state in the European Community without an official national buildings record. Its historic architecture, for the most part unprotected, was often unknown or unrecorded. Year by year historic buildings decayed and disappeared without any record being made for posterity. The architectural inheritance of the country wasted away with no inventory, either of the loss or of what was left. Founded by Edward McParland and Nicholas Robinson, the Irish Architectural Archive came into being in 1976 to supply these needs. With the support of An Taisce, and with financial assistance from the Heritage Trust, the Archive has now become the central body for the study of Irish historic architecture. It is an essential national resource with photographic and documentary records of over 20,000 buildings. It records – sometimes at very little notice – nationally important structures threatened with demolition. The Archive is also established as a research college for the study of Irish architecture and houses a collection of some 40,000 historical drawings.

The Irish Architectural Archive is a charitable company administered by a board of directors which includes architectural historians, architects and business people. *Ex officio* members of the board include the president of the Royal Institute of the Architects of Ireland and the secretary of the Royal Commission on Ancient and Historical Monuments of Scotland. Its staff cheerfully, and with great fortitude, cope with the pressures of an ever-increasing workload and the financial uncertainty attendant on a charitable undertaking that has yet to receive adequate state funding.

From the Archive's collections come the illustrations in this book. But the importance of the Irish Architectural Archive far transcends the collection of nostalgic views of what once was. For its task is also to survey what exists today, to evaluate it, to record it, and to help provide the informed and documented background to the Irish architectural heritage. Without this body of documentation, judgement and experience, planning would be mere whimsy. The time is right for a solution to the problems posed by the illustrations in this book. But it's our last chance.

1. Nat. Libr. Irl. MS 806, p. 49.

2. *Burke's Guide to Country Houses,* vol. 1. *Ireland.* 1978.

3. Despite its title, An Taisce plays a broad environmental watchdog role and has an important function as a prescribed   body under the Planning Acts. Its role as a property trust has always been marginal to its other functions and has almost certainly been restricted by these functions and by its public profile as a campaigning organisation.

4. Edited by Edward McParland and Nicholas Robinson.

5. Edited by Professor Kevin B. Nowlan and Lewis Clohessy.

6. Expressing the collective approach of the Heritage Trust, An Taisce, the Irish Historic Properties Committee,   the Irish Georgian Society and HITHA – the Historic Irish Tourist Houses and Gardens Association.

A PATCHWORK OF IRISH HOUSES

Desmond FitzGerald, Knight of Glin

The Bunsen burner flickered behind the counter of the cool, dark Limerick chemist's shop. Behind it was Stan Stewart, bespectacled at his counter poring over a one inch Ordnance Survey map. He was plotting a bicycle trip through County Clare meandering between dolmens and Romanesque churches, and looking forward perhaps to the prospect of cycling up the avenue of some decaying country house. I often found him studying these maps and seldom saw him dispensing his apothecaries' wares, a job he left to his brother Barney. This was in the late '40's when as a boy I escaped into his shop with its scent of soap and chemicals, relieved to get away from my mother who was left to her tedious shopping in the red brick Georgian streets of the town. Stan would show me tantalising photographs of old houses and ruins and it was he who kindled in me a life-long interest in architecture. He was also an intimate friend of Frank O'Connor, that brilliant Irish writer, and he proudly showed me two of O'Connors's Irish travel books, *Irish Miles* (1947) dedicated to Stan, and *Leinster, Munster, and Connacht* (1949), in which a number of Stan's architectural photographs appeared. O'Connor often turned to Stan in his hour of psychological need. Then they would go cycling together. These quirkey books glorify Romanesque churches and also show an appreciation for the buildings of the eighteenth century, not a fashionable field in the Ireland of the 1940's.

In *Irish Miles* O'Connor visited, probably in Stan's company, the shell of a great house called Mount Shannon just outside Limerick with its Ionic portico (Fig.1 – Facing: Photograph c.1955 by Standish Stewart.) and vast ranges of stables and farm buildings: 'Miles of stone wall which guarded the estate . . . were humped and rent by great clumps of ivy which straddled them and broke their back. We opened a ruined gate . . .' O'Connor goes on to describe the green peeling stucco of the Ionic front in the baleful yellow light of evening, the wilderness garden, and a meeting with an old countryman on his way home:

> ' ''Whose house was that?'' I asked.
>
> ''That was the house of Lord Clare''; he said, stopping.
> ''He was one time Lord Chancellor of Ireland. You might have heard of him?''
> ''I did'', said I.
> ''I saw his photograph knocked down at the auction here.
> Dressed in his robes and all. That was the greatest sale that was ever in these parts. I was only a
> boy at the time, but I saw them coming here from all parts, Jews and every sort. It went on for 8
> days . . .'' '

The countryman was amazed that a cup and saucer had been sold for £98 to a Limerick merchant prince and vividly described the house being burnt in 'the Troubles':

'There was a marble staircase that stretched the whole width of the house. It melted in the fire, and the melting lead pouring down on to it from the roof. It was a terrible sight! That was the finest house in this part of Ireland.'

Stan brought Frank O'Connor to many other houses near Limerick such as Mount Ievers, Co. Clare, one of the most magical of all Irish country houses, and Ballynaguarde near Ballyneety. Stan's photo of Ballynaguarde (Fig. 2), used in one of the two books *Leinster, Munster, and Connacht* shows a great stone statue of Hercules standing in front of the pedimented house with its gloomy shuttered windows. O'Connor wrote: 'there was a proposal to bring Hercules to Limerick, but a committee of inspection having studied him carefully fore and aft, decided that he would never do for the confraternities'!

I remember a sunny day when Stan took me to see all the houses round Castleconnell: Hermitage, Island House, Caherline and Mount Shannon itself. This ruin reminded him of Lord Chancellor Clare's famous

Fig. 2: *Ballinagarde, Co. Limerick: c.1949. The main facade with the statue of Hercules.*
Photograph: Standish Stewart. Copy photograph: David Davison.

words in his Union speech of 1800:

> 'The whole property of this country has been conferred by successive monarchs of England upon an English colony composed of three sets of English adventurers who poured into this country at the termination of three successive rebellions. Confiscation is their common title, and from their first settlement they have been hemmed in on every side by the old inhabitants of Ireland, brooding over their discontents in sullen indignation.'

The Lord Chancellor 'Black Jack' Fitzgibbon, knew what he was talking about and saw danger ahead. His family were decayed Catholic 'Old English' and had changed sides in the previous generation. Gerald Griffin, the local nineteenth century Limerick novelist, returns to this theme in the book *The Rivals* (1830). The Gaelic informer Tom Tobin, proud of his tattered pedigree, despises the English settlers whom he serves and calls the landlord living on his country estate a man of low extraction;

> 'of no family. And yet 'tis such fellows that live in such Elysiums as this, while the Blakes, the O'Donnells, the FitzGeralds, the Butlers . . . the McCarthys . . . and all the cream and top of the old Irish nobility are scattered over the country, hedging and ditching and tilling, as hired laborers, the lands which their ancestors won in fight, and held father to son at the point of the sword.'

These sentiments help us to understand the Irish attitude towards Ireland's 'ascendancy' families and their great houses, and even Yeats with his obsession with the Anglo-Irish realised only too well the world within and without the great demesne walls. For instance in his poem in memory of the Gore-Booth sisters he talks of their great house Lissadell in Sligo:

> '*we* the great gazebo built,
> *they* convicted us of guilt' (author's italics)

Lady Fingall in her memoirs echoes this feeling when reminiscing about her own lost Galway home Danesfield: 'the front of the house seems to have had a blank look, the windows staring across the country, like blind eyes. It is a look that the windows of Irish country houses often have, as though indeed that was the spirit of the colonists and conquerors, looking out across the country which they possessed, but never owned.' Later when she became the chatelaine of Killeen Castle (Fig. 3), County Meath, home of one of the only titled Irish Catholic families, she rejoiced in the fact that the Earls of Fingall spent so much money on their great baronial castle that they built no demesne wall around it 'keeping Ireland and the people out'. She often thought what a lovely ruin it would make and Killeen, empty for many years was burnt recently and so joins the long roll of lost houses which this book memorialises.

Another burning, this time by mistake, was at Harristown, County Kildare in 1891 and here lived Ruskin's friend Mrs. John La Touche, the mother of Rose La Touche. Mrs. La Touche was a highly intelligent sensitive woman and found little in common with her hard riding, hunting neighbours in that most sporting of counties. She took the burning of so many beautiful things with quiet resignation, and while her husband rebuilt the house, they moved to a cottage near her entrance gate. A friend of hers wrote:

> 'To my suprise she quite welcomed being brought more on a level with average human beings, seeing

them pass her windows and becoming acquainted with them and their lives. While staying in that cottage, she said to me one day, she doubted much if it were right to "live at the end of long avenues far away from one's fellow creatures".'

Many years later Elizabeth Bowen agonised over the isolation of the long avenue – Irish houses are a series of remote islands in the melancholy countryside. She wrote in an essay, 'The Big House' (1940) that it was not so much isolation as mystery, and these places with their ring of woods were a *bois-dormant* each under its individual spell. Virginia Woolf sourly described Bowen's Court (Fig. 4) as:

'merely a great stone box, but full of Italian mantlepieces and decayed 18th century furniture, and carpets in holes – however they insisted upon keeping up a ramshackle kind of state, dressing for dinner and so on'.

It was however true to say that in Ireland grandeur and poverty often walked hand-in-hand. Elizabeth Bowen's life at Bowen's Court inspired those tragic unsurpassed annals of an Irish family before the house met the fate of demolition at the hands of a local farmer. The attitudes of Lady Fingall and Elizabeth Bowen show an awareness of the social and ancestral differences in a country of many racial origins. In their ability to express the subtleties of their class's predicament they were relatively rare. The landowning class were in general incapable or unwilling to admit the uneasiness of their place in Irish life – religion, folk memories

Fig. 3: *Killeen Castle, Co. Meath: The entrance front c.1970.*
Photograph: Alistair Rowan.

and even language underlined the dichotomy of their existence.

At home in County Limerick Stan Stewart's expeditions became a cheerful fixture of my adolescence, and after seeing that evocative picture of Hercules outside the gaunt tumble-down Ballynaguarde I was tempted to visit the place to see if any other statuary were left. Lying in a field a headless Andromeda chained to her rock was discovered near a clump of nettles, bought for £1 and triumphantly brought back to Glin. Her curvacious marble form now decorates the summer house in the walled garden.

These great houses had a kind of fascination for the country people and the sexual exploits of the landlord were a particularly favoured subject for gossip. In many cases this folklore mistakes one generation for another. Sean Feehan recounts with a lascivious pleasure in *The Magic of the Shannon* (1980), the tale of the early nineteenth-century Lord Lorton whose estate cottages at Rockingham lacked back doors, so that the poor peasant girls as a result could never make their escape from the embraces of their landlord. In actual fact the 1st Lord Lorton was the spirit of rectitude, and the story harks back to a libertine and rascally Lord Kingsborough who lived in the rakehell mid-eighteenth century. Christopher French St. George of Tyrone, County Galway built a charming little Gothic castle at Kilcolgan for his *chère amie* in Regency times, not far from that great ruined block Tyrone with its haughty cut stone facade overloaded with ornament that

Fig. 4: *Bowen's Court, Co. Cork: The entrance hall c.1930.*
Photograph: Collection Mrs. Simms. Copy photograph: David Davison.

Fig. 5: *Tyrone House, Co. Galway: The entrance front c.1870.*

today backs blankly across the landscape to Galway Bay (Fig. 5). This house and its family history was of course the inspiration for Somerville and Ross's epic: *The Big House at Inver* (1925). Many noblemen, like the heroes of mythology were credited with great sexual prowess and at another Galway estate, Portumna Castle, the first Marquess of Clanricarde was well known for his amorous exploits in company with his henchman Tom Nolan known as 'Tom the devil'. In 1836 a man nearly died at a drunken orgy in a neighbouring Galway house, and the descriptions of these riotous days sound just like a passage from a novel by Charles Lever – novels that are peopled by a squirearchy well described in Charles Macklin's play *The Trueborn Irishman* (1783): 'a damn'd honest, rory-tory, rantum-scantum, daring, singing, laughing, boozing, friendly, fighting, hospitable people'. Pride and touchiness led to duels, and drink and womanising were all part of their character.

At Glin my ancestor John Fraunceis FitzGerald, though quite a scholarly and well educated man, had a series of kept women in cottages on the estate much to the chagrin of the local priest, 'who did much to curb the oriental proclivities of his aristocratic neighbour' as a local historian, Archdeacon Begley puts it. The Earl of Glengall was always said to have used the Swiss Cottage in Cahir Park, now being so triumphantly restored, for the same amorous purposes. John B. Keane commenting recently on the outlandish stories about sexual exploits that are discussed in small country towns tells us that 'golf clubs have replaced the great houses as places of scandal-making and sexual orgies'!

What were these Irish houses generally like? In answer, I shall refer to a number of contemporary descriptions culled from a series of memoirs and reminiscences.

Limerick had its fair share of old houses and as soon as I could persuade anyone to drive me I would visit them in my holidays. Many of them were crumbling away like Riddlestown Park, a tall early Georgian box of fine proportions with a high roof and big brick chimneys. Its interior has been livelily painted in about 1880 by Sir William Nott Bower, who as a young police officer was stationed in Rathkeale, the nearby town. He was very friendly with the owners, the Blennerhassett family, and he wrote:

'The large entrance hall was filled with tables, littered with newspapers, novels, hunting crops, walking sticks, hats and coats, in endless confusion; chairs with broken legs and rickety cabinets loaded with priceless china, never cared for, and never dusted. The household consisted of only two or three good natured, but absolutely inefficient servants, though devoted to the "ould" family. At Riddlestown there was always the most cordial of welcomes and the truest hospitality – the best of everything that was going, a good bottle of claret after dinner, which was at once whipped off the table the moment the ladies disappeared and replaced by a bowl of steaming whiskey punch. The one thing always lacking was "money", but that did not seem to affect life.'

Riddlestown is a simpler version of Richard Castle's Waterston, County Westmeath (Fig. 6) which is charmingly described in Eyre Crowe's novel *Today in Ireland* (1825), and as this description fits so many Irish houses I shall quote it in full:

'It was a solid square building of dark granite, richly ornamented, of almost perpendicular roof, and chimneys of enormous size. It exactly resembled one of the extreme wings, or *pavilions* as they are called, of the

Tuileries, the height of the roof and chimney not perhaps so exaggerated; and had Plunketstown, (Waterston in the novel) been ornamented with the *jalousies* of the *Pavillon de Flore* . . . the model had been exact. A huge flight of steps, descending, like a waterfall from a central point in the front towards the lawn, was an indispensable appendix; whilst a deep fosse, running quite around the house attempted to attain the security of the ancient castle, without infringing upon the commodiousness of the modern dwelling.'

The interior of a far grander house than Riddlestown, Dromana, County Waterford, now mostly demolished was described in rather similar terms in the Autumn of 1836, from a diary of her mother quoted in Gertrude Lyster's *Family Chronicle* (1908):

'Dromana is quite beautiful! The house is built on a rock overhanging the Blackwater − you might drop a stone out of the drawing-room windows through the trees into the water . . . The house is (like all things in Ireland) full of contrasts − such a grand drawing-room, such tumble-down offices, sixteen lamps in the chandelier, and pack-thread for bell ropes; a beautiful gold paper, and no curtains to the six windows; an eagle before the windows, a stuffed seal in the hall, some great elk horns over the staircase, lots of family pictures, an old theatre turned into a workshop, the remains of what must have been very fine hanging gardens, connected by stone steps, down to the river.'

Going back to 1807 a German, J.F. Hering, travelling in Connacht noted that when he was invited to the big country house of a rich landowner − we do not know its name or where the house was, except that

Fig. 6: *Waterston, Co. Westmeath: The garden front c.1910.*

Fig. 7: *Kilballyowen, Co. Limerick: The drawing room c.1965.*   *Photograph: Lord Rossmore.*

Fig. 8: *Kilballyowen, Co. Limerick: The hall chimneypiece c.1965.* Photograph: Lord Rossmore.

it was very dilapidated:

> 'the front steps had fallen in, the interior was rich but neglected, for example the large silk window and bed curtains were in tatters, and had certainly not been dusted for many years. As for the rest, the household furniture was of English make and the dining-table was overflowing'.

Two houses in County Limerick which were very much in this vein were Kilballyowen the seat of an Irish chieftain, The O'Grady, and Tervoe, which belonged to the Monsells, previously Lords Emly. To a youthful eye, Kilballyowen was particularly magnificent – resplendent with its French wallpaper and elaborate festooned borders in the drawing-room (Fig. 7). This huge room with its three long windows was draped with the elaborate remains of Empire style curtains. In the hall (Fig. 8), there was a cut stone chimney-piece and the obligatory Irish elk horns, guns, and a tattered banner of the Volunteers decorated the walls. A door led to the staircase and the bedroom floor where every bedroom had a draped four poster bed all in an advanced state of decay. I brought the photographer Lord Rossmore there in the 1960's and his photographs of these rooms are now the only record of the house before its total demolition. Stan Stewart accompanied me first to Tervoe with its oval drawing-room hung with painted panels, and another drawing-room with plaster plaques after Thorvaldson inset over the doors (Fig. 9). Rows of portraits and gilt framed flower prints by Thornton and

Fig. 9: *Tervoe, Co. Limerick: Drawing room c.1945.*   *Photograph: Standish Stewart.*

Fig. 10: *Springfield Castle, Co. Limerick: The dining room c.1890.*

Fig. 11: *Moore Hall, Co. Mayo: The ruined entrance front c.1965.*   *Photograph: Lord Rossmore.*

other priceless works of art were all in an advanced state of dilapidation from the damp. Commander Monsell the owner, according to Mark Bence-Jones, smoking innumerable cigars, retreated from room to room as ceilings yielded progressively to the rain. Eventually the house was gutted and I persuaded my mother to buy two splendid marble chimney-pieces and the painted panels and plaster plaques were thrown in for nothing.

Sunday lunches were often spent visiting Springfield Castle, County Limerick, the home of Lord and Lady Muskerry. His lordship had worked as a jackeroo in Australia and inherited the property from a distant cousin, rebuilding the house after it had been burnt in 'the Troubles'. The wife of the previous Lord Muskerry was Catholic, and it is said that she took her Pekinese to mass one Sunday which so incensed the locals that they burnt down the house; the old Springfield had a dining-room decorated with delicate neoclassical plaster work, and I was shown an old photograph of this room (Fig. 10) taken in late Victorian times with an elaborate table setting and heavy oak Jacobean Revival chairs. There is something very evocative about such photographs and I have always made a point of searching for them ever since. Suprised owners have to drag out from forgotten cupboards old albums recording the social round of Victorian and Edwardian visits. These often yield many records of house parties showing houses in the background which have now totally disappeared. Many have been re-photographed and carefully stored and catalogued in the Irish Architectural Archive.

It is suprising how many unfamiliar memoirs and tours there are which mention Irish houses, and of course the literature on 'the Big House' is immense – Irish novelists like Lady Morgan, Maturin, Lover, Lever, Carleton and many others, like Thackeray and Trollope have written much which bears on the subject. Authors such as Molly Keane, Jennifer Johnston and William Trevor to mention but three have fed the current hunger for aristocratic nostalgia. Maria Edgeworth's *Castle Rackrent* (1800) and *The Absentee* (1809) are particularly brilliant examples of this genre. Her tours in Ireland are not so well known. In the autumn of 1836 Maria and her party set off for Moore Hall, Co. Mayo (Fig. 11) to visit Mr. and Mrs. George Moore, the famous novelist's grandparents. Her description shows that not all remote Irish houses were examples of barbaric decay. Though on their way they got lost in bog roads of incomparable 'cowpatishness', they arrived just in time for a very late dinner:

> 'To my astonishment' she wrote, 'I found Moore Hall which I had fancied would be a dilapidated ree-raw wild kind of hand to mouth house and establishment, a most excellent house, beautifully furnished in the best taste and with all the comforts and luxuries of life, in dining-room – bedrooms – library – drawing-room. The library especially a most livable and elegant literary room – papered with a sort of gothic paper representing a colonnade of pillars and fretwork arches above and all manner of tables and armchairs and low and highbacks – springing and rolling – bookcases with networked doors opening easily – no higher than you can reach – books well chosen – all round two rooms; for this library opened into a study of Mr. Moore's with a snuggery and charming writing desk for himself.
>
> 'The summer drawing-room papered with green trellis paper, the prettiest I ever saw, large windows to the ground opening on balcony from which you see from the eminence on which the house stands a clear spreading lake below – wooded and islanded – and with a sort of jutting spoon shaped cape. The house and plantations are on a peninsula.'

George Moore, the writer, loved and hated that house. In *A Story-Tellers Holiday* (1928) he fretted about the lifting of its roof by his father, and the replacement of its 'green mortared slates – like scales' with large blue modern ones; he sadly bewailed the plate glass windows that were substituted for the small panes, 'with eyes in them like grease spots on soup'. These aesthetic reflections did not overcome a strange aversion. He was, as he put it, 'diffident, shy, ill at ease, at Moore Hall' and 'ashamed, frightened, overcome by the awe that steals over one in the presence of the dead'. He called Moore Hall 'a relic, a ruin, a corpse', and very soon it was to become just this, as it was burnt down in 1923. Moore had a great poetic feeling towards old houses and this is nowhere better illustrated than in his descriptions in *Hail and Farewell* (1947) of Mount Venus above Rathfarnham on the way to the Dublin mountains. He talks of the beautiful grove of beech trees and 'the resolute house, emphatic as an oath, with great steps before the door, and each made out of a single stone, a house at which one knocks timidly, less mastiffs would rush out, eager for the strangling'.

Returning to some of those tours which illustrate life in Irish houses, the famous diary of Thomas Creevey records a visit to his great friends the Ponsonby family, Earls of Bessborough, in September 1828, where he admired the gray stone Palladian house with its terrace and fine situation. Bessborough, Co. Kilkenny was also burnt in 'the Troubles' but rebuilt and is now an institution. Creevey informs us:

> 'The history of this family may be said to be the history of ill fated Ireland. Duncannon's great grandfather began building this house in 1745, he finished it in 1755, and lived in it 'till 1757 (two years), when he died. His son left Ireland when 18 years old, and having never seen it more, died in 1792. Upon that event his son, the present Lord Bessborough, made his first visit to the place, and he is not certain whether it was *two* or *three* days he stayed here, but it was one or the other. In 1808, he and Lady Bessborough came on a tour to *the Lake of Killarney*, and having taken their own house in their way either going or coming, they were so pleased with it as to stay here a *week*, and once more in 1812 having come over to see the young Duke of Devonshire at Lismore, when his Father died, they were here a month. So that from 1757 to 1825, 68 years, the family was (here) 5 weeks and 2 days . . . My dears, it is absenteeism on the part of landlords, and the havoc that middlemen make with their property that plays the very devil . . .'

Later he visited Knocklofty, Killarney House, Woodstock, Carton and spent a considerable time in Dublin. His diary is well worth reading as he had an ironic sense of humour, and a brilliant and perceptive sense of people's character. At Woodstock (Fig. 12), now a romantic shell, he was amazed by the haughty Duchess of Richmond who never spoke to her Irish son-in-law because he was an Irishman, and who continued her silence though she was quite prepared to stay three months in his house!

A contemporary of Creevey also in Ireland in 1828 was the German Prince von Pückler Muskau who besides being an heiress-hunter had a passion for landscape gardening and visiting country mansions. Most houses both in England and Ireland of any stature were opened to any interested party as long as they had a sufficiently respectable carriage. He was, however, refused admittance at Kilruddery, Co. Wicklow but saw the glories of Bellevue with its vast ranges of glass houses; Castle Howard too opened its doors to him. He went on to Shelton Abbey but Powerscourt maddeningly was closed on Sundays which the Prince thought shocking. Later he visited many other houses such as Glengarriff Castle, Co. Cork, the seat of Lord Bantry's brother, Colonel White who was a devoted 'parkomane' as he put it, like himself. At Mitchelstown Castle (Fig. 13) he was unimpressed by its grandeur calling it 'a huge heap of stone which has cost its possessor

Fig. 12: *Woodstock, Co. Kilkenny: Entrance front 1864.*
Photograph: Augusta Crofton, Gillman Coll. Copy photograph: David Davison.

Fig. 13: *Mitchelstown Castle, Co. Cork: A general view of the White Knight's tower c.1870.*
Photograph: Gillman Collection. Copy photograph: David Davison.

£50,000' but which was not in good taste, and he waxes withering about its confused style and unimpressive park. Colonel White's little castle was, he thought, infinitely preferable and built at an eighth of the cost. Mitchelstown's interiors, complete with grand stairs and long gallery, he considered no better and a visit could be disposed of in 5 minutes! To cap Pückler Muskau's disastrous tour the key of the White Knight's tower with its famous view was nowhere to be found.

Alexis de Tocqueville the French political commentator visited Mitchelstown a few years later in the summer of 1835. The Earl had gone off his head and the estate was by then burdened with debts of £400,000. The catholic de Tocqueville comments: 'It is like that almost everywhere in Ireland, witness the finger of God. The Irish aristocracy wanted to remain separated from the people and still be English. It has driven itself into imitating the English aristocracy without possessing either its skill or its resources, and its own sin is proving its ruin.' Mitchelstown has now been totally demolished and only miles of the usual ivy clad wall tell us of its previous pretentious existence. The intrepid Prince went on to Cahir, Thomastown – now a romantic ruin – Malahide and Howth. All these houses were easily accessible to the curious traveller.

Later in the century in 1865 John Thadeus Delane, the famous editor of *The Times,* who was of Irish extraction, visited Ireland and stayed at Shanbally. This was Lord Lismore's magnificent castle (Fig. 14), designed by Nash in 1806 at a cost of £90,000 and furnished throughout by Gillow. The gardens were immaculately kept and he saw six gardeners on the lawns as he wrote a letter to Walter Dasent. Conversation with his host Lord Lismore was all about the Fenians and it was from the 1860's onwards that we find the land wars beginning, which rang the death knell of the Irish aristocracy. A series of Land Acts ensued which opened the way to the shearing of thousands of acres from many estates. It was not so much the financial loss to the landlord which was the problem, as they were well compensated by the British Government. It was an emotional loss. Landlords who once presided over thousands of acres of tenant farms, now found themselves bound by the perimeter walls of their own demesnes. All this took place in an Ireland in which rapid changes were happening politically and administratively, to the detriment of the influence and standing of the landed classes. Eventually these houses were stranded hulks in an utterly altered environment. It would prove to be the end of one period of Irish landlordism.

Delane also visited Killarney House, the old early Georgian high-gabled building that preceded George Devey's great red brick extravaganza of 1877/1880 and he wrote on October 22 1865:

> 'Yesterday Castlerosse took us in a six oared boat through all the three lakes, lunching us at one point, tea-ing us at another, and ending with a dinner of sixteen, served in a manner which could not be surpassed in Belgrave Square. Certainly so as far as I have seen the Irish country houses are very superior in their style and their establishments . . .'

Our series of quotations have shown us that there was a great variety of household arrangements varying from the grand cosmopolitan Irish aristocratic grandees down to the less well off and often improvident squirearchy. The life and times of this class have never been entirely chronicled. Mark Bence-Jones's recent book *Twilight of the Ascendancy* tells us much of the social life of the last hundred years or so but the eighteenth and early nineteenth century needs a book to bring Constantia Maxwell's great work about the country up to date. It is not a popular subject today as many Irishmen will echo the views of Louis McNeice when considering the inmates of Ireland's aristocratic world: 'In most cases these houses maintain no culture worth speaking of – nothing but an obsolete bravado, an insidious bonhomie and a way with horses.' It should be noted that the horse was the main bond with the plain people of Ireland and crossed all social and religious boundaries. The country people might find it easier to talk to this class than to the business tycoon of today!

Yeats tried to create an apologia for this Anglo-Irish race but in truth no real generalisations can be made until a greater study takes place of individual families, their collecting activities, their books, their pictures and intellectual life. Patrick Melvin who has been doing this for Co. Galway has gathered together a great deal of material about the enormous number of houses that used to be there, almost all of which are now in ruins or have disappeared. This subject needs to be further extended throughout Ireland.

Fig. 14: *Shanbally Castle, Co. Tipperary: Garden front during demolition c.1957.*

Speaking of the Irish aristocracy Professor George O'Brien writes:

'They adored the country that hated them in return: they idolized the people who ridiculed them. They never could understand why they were unpopular. They were willing to give devoted service when it was not wanted. They simply could not understand that their neighbours despised the idols that they held sacred. Their own dual loyalty to England and Ireland was incomprehensible to the people by whom they were surrounded. They were nationalists in a fashion of their own. Their nationalism was set in a wider imperial loyalty . . .

Turning to their relations with catholicism he continues 'they never understood each other. Ireland would have been a very different and vastly poorer country if it had not experienced the impact of these two great imperial civilizations . . . but each failed to understand the value of the other's contribution'.

The great and small country houses that survive today remind us and tell us something of the class which has been almost swept away. Some houses are sophisticated and architect designed, and others are pattern book bumpkin essays of much charm. These survivors are all the more important when one sees that according to this book, about five hundred have disappeared or are in ruins. I am not suggesting that all that are left can be preserved, because not many in these days can afford to live in them or keep them up. The smaller ones near Dublin easily find new owners and the grandest of the grand elsewhere occasionally lure international private buyers or become hotels. What is really vital is that the few owned by the original families and which still contain many of their contents such as portraits, furniture and memorabilia should be encouraged to survive because they represent an important element of Irish history. If no life line is thrown out to them soon, they will all drown in a decade or so.

The need to preserve buildings of outstanding natural beauty or of national, historical, and scientific importance has had much lip service in Ireland over the years. Recent forward looking tax advantages have been provided. What has not been adequately perceived is the considerable commercial value to the nation of holding and administering such properties for the future. If we are to sell Ireland abroad over the coming decade in the tourist market which is currently our second most important industry, we must appreciate the very real economic contribution made by property owning National Trusts all over Europe. These places if properly used should not only create jobs locally but be the inspiration for the teaching of history and the study of Irish craftsmanship. Even if the upper classes were considered 'foreign', the craftsmen and the builders were Irishmen. The naive assumption that these houses are to be seen as merely memorials to outdated colonialism should be resisted because they are in fact treasure houses of Irish skills.

Oliver St. John Gogarty, in an aptly named chapter called 'The destruction still goes on' in *Rolling down the Lea* (1950), remarks that since childhood he had heard laments for the losses of our manuscripts, goldsmiths' work and ancient monuments. These losses were attributed to the Danes but he mentions uncovering the culprits in a much more recent period and bewails the losses of irreplaceable mansions by the shortsighted policies of De Valera's era. In the United States, homes of great men and their records were carefully preserved and collected. In this context he strongly regretted the loss of Delville, Co. Dublin (Fig. 15), with its literary associations centred round Dean Delany, his famous diarist wife, Swift and Stella. Another example is Coole

Fig. 15: *Delville, Co. Dublin:*
The Eating Parlour c.1950.
Photograph: Phyllis Thompson.
Copy photograph: David Davison.

Park (Fig. 16), where Lady Gregory's circle included the poet Yeats. The Bon Secours Hospital at Glasnevin replaces Delville, the house at Coole was demolished and the demesne and its Seven Woods largely split up. Gogarty writes 'Someone, not unmindful of the fate of Coole, bought its hall-door for five pounds ($12). From it he cut a heart-shaped piece of wood which held the knocker. This he offered to the Dublin Municipal Gallery. It was refused because, no doubt, those who conducted a gallery of Ireland's great did not want such a stultifying reminder of the many acts of vandalism against ''the noblest of the things that are gone'' '. Gogarty was a voice crying in the drab wilderness of his time.

The recent sale of Mount Juliet, Co. Kilkenny, caused a certain flurry in the press and Hugh Montgomery Massingberd wrote recently in *The Sunday Telegraph*: 'The urgent need is clear for a state funded body with the muscle to own nationally important properties, to administer grants and generally streamline the preservation of Ireland's heritage.'

Fig. 16: *Coole Park, Co. Galway: Lady Gregory at her desk in the drawing room c.1920.*
Photograph by George Bernard Shaw.
Reproduced by kind permission of the Society of Authors on behalf of the Shaw Estate. From a print by Colin Smythe.

Kevin Myers, a latter day diarist in *The Irish Times*, further considering the problem of Mount Juliet wrote with greater strength and passion than anyone as partisan as myself could do:

'The day is not far ahead when the work of the Republic will be complete and not a single great country house stands in this State. The triumphs of the 18th century will have been obliterated; Palladian mansions will be reduced to unaccountable rubble in neglected parklands; fine stands of trees which were mature when Goldsmith and Berkeley and Sheridan illuminated the world will be felled to make way for one of the ornaments of the Republic, mock-Georgian Spanish South Fork-type bungalows; and countless masters and lesser works will have found their way on to distant walls in strange countries leaving no trace behind that once they adorned Irish houses.

And by then the process of rewriting history will be complete and the 18th century will be recalled merely as a time of unrelieved unpleasantness which left no traceable worthwhile monument on the Irish landscape. Walls will fall into ruins; ivy will conceal the remnants; grass will break through and vanquish ancient driveways. And then we shall be the glory of all of Europe – a country with no intermediate history between the triumphs of the Gael and the triumphs of the Gaelic revival.

We are uncomfortably close to that bleak and pagan epoch. In the last year, castle after castle, great house after great house have come up on the market. Properties which should have passed on to the custodianship of a caring State have fallen into disrepair; others have languished waiting for a buyer.

In poor unfortunate Northern Ireland, groaning under the iniquity of British tyranny, such great houses would come under the care of the National Trust and would be open to tourists and give employment and so on. Happily, the proud Republic is spared such indignities. We have our rubble.'

Fighting words indeed; we can only hope that a broader vision towards this part of our heritage will occur before it is too late. It is quite illuminating to see the attitudes of another journalist Nuala O'Faolain writing in the *The Irish Times* about the rebirth of the great Palladian house at Strokestown Co. Roscommon. After rehearsing the vast acres originally owned by the King Harman and Mahon families, their horses, Chippendale bookcases, hot houses, ornamental lakes, London houses etc., she goes on to say 'every particle of their wealth (was) extracted from the Irish peasantry' and she talks about the great houses in which they lived their lives of strenuous leisure. We burnt them down 'Ill gotten, ill gone' . . . the lads must have muttered as they crept across the weedy demesnes with burning brands in their hands. Today at Strokestown you pay your fee to no landlord but to contribute towards the restoration of the house and though Ms. O'Faolain still feels it impossible to look at these houses without a degree of rage she concedes: 'there is no point sulking about history. Better to embrace such legacies as we've got'. By the end of her article she is full of admiration for the restoration and the imaginative educational role that Strokestown will have for future generations.

It is hoped that this book with its melancholy catalogue of loss may help to influence our legislators, whatever their political leanings, to see the stark reality of the present day situation and through some funding from central government or the State Lottery, set up adequate machinery for the survival of some of our major houses and their contents for Ireland's posterity.

The English poet Sir John Betjeman fell in love with Ireland's romantic decay, its ruined houses and obscure members of the Irish peerage when visiting the Longford family at Pakenham Hall, Co. Westmeath in the 1930's. He wrote his famous poem 'Sir John Piers' and it was first published by the *Westmeath Examiner* in 1938. During one of his visits to Westmeath he took this poignant photograph (Fig. 17) of the tottering cantilevered staircase in the disintegrating shell of Portleman originally the seat of the de Blaquieres, a house and family poetically mentioned in this epic. The photograph sums up the theme of this book with a devastating and tragic clarity and perhaps a fitting end piece to this essay should be a couple of verses from another of Betjeman's Irish poems 'The Small Towns of Ireland':

'But where is his lordship who once in a phaeton
Drove out twixt his lodges and into the town?
Oh his tragic misfortune I will not dilate on;
His mansions a ruin, his woods are cut down.

His impoverished descendent is dwelling in Ealing,
His daughters must type for their bread and their board,
O'er the graves of his forbears the nettle is stealing
And few will remember the sad Irish Lord.'

Should we not remember and preserve some of this important aspect of our national inheritance?

Fig. 17: *Portleman, Co. Westmeath: The cantilevered staircase in dereliction c.1935.*
Photograph: Sir John Betjeman. Copy photograph: David Davison.

County Lists of Vanishing Houses
in the
Republic of Ireland

David J. Griffin

In the lists which follow the houses are arranged alphabetically under each county, and all houses mentioned in the book are listed in the general index.

These lists make no claim to be exhaustive and this is especially true of the houses in the suburbs of Dublin, Cork and other large towns, but it is hoped that they include most of the more important losses of the last hundred years or so.

Included are houses completely demolished, in ruins, unoccupied for a long period and also houses where the most important portion of the building has been demolished such as Dromana, Co. Waterford, Glendalough House, Co. Wicklow, and Springfield Castle, Co. Limerick. Rossanagh, Co. Wicklow, the main block of which survives, is included because of the loss of its most important interior, the magnificent panelled saloon in one of the demolished wings.

Dates of destruction are given where known.

See Authorities for *A Patchwork of Irish Houses* following Index.

COUNTY CARLOW

BALLIN TEMPLE, Tullow
A large, three storey, mid to late eighteenth-century house, to which a fine single storey Greek Doric portico was added on the entrance front in the early nineteenth century. The house which was destroyed by fire, stood as a shell for many years before being demolished. The seat of the Butler family in the late nineteenth century.

BALLYTIMON, Fennagh
Simple, two storey, granite faced, early nineteenth-century house. Derelict.

BURTON HALL, Carlow
An important early eighteenth-century house begun in 1712. The house was originally of three storeys, but the top floor was removed in the late nineteenth century before 1896. The house was sold by the Burton family in 1927 and the main block was demolished in 1930.
A small wing remains.

CLOGRENANE, Carlow
A large early nineteenth-century house built by the Rochfort family. Now a ruin.

DUCKETT'S GROVE, Carlow
A huge and impressive Gothic fantasy castle, designed by Thomas A. Cobden in 1830 for John Dawson Duckett, incorporating an early eighteenth-century house. The house was destroyed by fire in 1933. The shell still survives as a magnificent ruin.

HANOVER HOUSE, Carlow
An early eighteenth-century gable-ended house with a pedimented breakfront. The segmental-headed doorcase with keystone was similar to those in the upper castle yard, Dublin Castle. Demolished.

KILCOLTRIM, Borris
A very interesting eighteenth-century house, now a ruin with a severe doorcase and two massive chimney-stacks. The stone central cantilevered staircase remains intact. The house is similar to Summer Grove, Co. Leix, in that the back half has an extra floor fitted into the same overall height as the front. The seat of the Hegarty family in the late nineteenth century.

KILDAVIN HOUSE, Clonegall
Small, two storey, gable-ended, early nineteenth-century house. Built for Beauch Colclough. Derelict.

KILNOCK HOUSE, Ballon
A large, three storey, eighteenth-century house with flanking two storey wings, much altered and extended in the late nineteenth and early twentieth centuries. Demolished 1940

KNOCKDUFF, St. Mullins
Early eighteenth-century gable-ended house, the entrance front has a steep pediment and exceptionally small windows with moulded sills. Unoccupied.

POLLACTON, Carlow
A large somewhat severe house designed by Richard Morrison in 1803 for Sir Charles Burton. The interior however was very attractive and contained plasterwork by James Talbot. Demolished 1970.

RUSSELLSTOWN PARK, Carlow
A two storey classical house built in 1824 to the design of Thomas Cobden for the Duckett family. Demolished, but a good gate lodge survives.

ST. AUSTIN'S ABBEY, Tullow
Designed by Sir Thomas Newenham Deane and Benjamin Woodward 1858-1859 for Charles Henry Doyne. The house was burnt *c.*1921 and the ruin has since been partly demolished. The stable block and some fragments of the house still remain.

Facing page:
Pollacton: Entrance hall 1970.
Photograph: David Davison.

Above:

St. Austin's Abbey.
Photograph c.1860. Gillman Collection. Copy photograph: David Davison.

Right:

Hanover House: Entrance front c.1975.
Photograph: William Garner.

Facing page:

Burton Hall: Entrance front before removal of top floor, and garden front before removal of top floor.
Victorian photographs.

Duckett's Grove: Entrance front.
Old photograph. Copy photograph: David Davison.

Duckett's Grove: In ruins.
Photograph: Lord Rossmore.

COUNTY CAVAN

ANNAGHLEE, Cootehill
Very attractive and interesting small house with a good interior attributed to Richard Castle built *c.*1750 for Robert Wills. Now almost completely ruined.

ASHFIELD LODGE, Cootehill
A two storey, late-Georgian, bow fronted house. The seat of the Clements family. Sold in 1952.   Demolished.

CLOVERHILL, Belturbet
Designed *c.*1797 for James Sanderson by Francis Johnston possibly incorporating an earlier house. Derelict.

FORT FREDERICK, Virginia
Two storey mid Georgian home for the Sankey family. Gothic doorcase. Nineteenth-century timber porch.   Demolished.

LISAGOAN, Ballyhaise
Interesting, well planned, two storey, classical house of *c.*1810. Stone tripartite doorcase with oval window above (which may originally have been Diocletian) all recessed in an arch. Built as the dower house to Ballyhaise for the Humphrys family. Now a ruin.

LISMORE, Crossdoney
A house dating from *c.*1730 and attributed to Sir Edward Lovett Pearce. This house was very much in the style of Sir John Vanburgh, his cousin. The house became a ruin in this century and the central block except for one tower was demolished *c.*1952. The flanking pavilions still remain.

STRADONE HOUSE, Stradone
Large classical house designed in 1828 by John B. Keane for Major F. Burrows.   Demolished.

Lismore: Entrance front.
Photograph c.1880.

Above:
Lisagoan: Detail of entrance front c.1975.
Photograph: William Garner.

Top right:
Annaghlee: Entrance front c.1955.
Photograph: Maurice Craig.

Bottom right:
Clover Hill: Entrance front c.1975.
Photograph: William Garner.

COUNTY CLARE

BALLYCANNON HOUSE, Ardnacrusha
A two storey Tudor Revival house.   Demolished 1963.

BALLYGRIFFEY, Ennis
Early nineteenth-century 'castle' in ruins.

BELVOIR, Sixmilebridge
An early nineteenth-century Tudor Revival house built for David Wilson with a single storey porch. Attached chapel built 1862-1863 still in use.   Now a ruin.

BIRCHFIELD, Liscannor
Early nineteenth-century castellated house built for Cornelius O'Brien. Symmetrical entrance front with octagonal towers at each end.   Now a ruin.

CASTLE CRINE, Sixmilebridge
Castellated late Georgian house. Seat of the Crine family. Demolished 1950. Gothic gate lodge in ruins.

CLONBOY, Bridgetown
A two storey, pedimented, early nineteenth-century house. Seat of the Brown family.   Demolished in the 1940's.

CLOONEY, Ennis
A two storey, pedimented, mid nineteenth-century house with single storey porch. Seat of the Bindon family and probably the birth place of Francis Bindon, the architect.   Now a ruin.

CORNFIELD, Ballinacally
Built for Westropp Ross, J.P.
Demolished. A good barn with slit windows remains.

CULLAUN CASTLE, Sixmilebridge
Three bay, two storey house built c.1820 for the Steele family. Now a ruin.

DRUMCONORA, Ennis
A large, three storey, pedimented, mid to late eighteenth-century house. In 1786 the seat of the Crow family.   Demolished.

FENLOE HOUSE, Newmarket-on-Fergus
Three bay, two storey, early nineteenth-century house with a

cut stone shouldered doorcase. Seat of the Hickmans. Now a ruin.

FINNEVARA HOUSE, Burren
A two storey, eighteenth-century, gable-ended house. Entrance front with Venetian windows.   Now a ruin.

FORTFERGUS, Killadysert
Long, two storey, Georgian house with Tudor Revival chimney-stacks. Seat of John Stacpoole in 1800.
Destroyed by fire in 1922.

HAZLEWOOD, Quin
A large, two storey, late Georgian house with single storey porch which was a later addition. Former seat of the Studdert family. Burnt in 1921.   Demolished.

KILLADERRY HOUSE, Broadford
A two storey, early eighteenth-century, gable-ended house. Oculus over front door. Seat of the Bentleys in the 1720's. Demolished before 1900.

KILTANON, Tulla
Three storey Georgian house with its main cornice at second floor level. Seat of the Molonys for seven generations.
Destroyed by fire in 1930's.

LISMEHANE, O'Callaghan's Mills
A large early eighteenth-century house built for John Westropp. Refaced and altered c.1880, these alterations included the addition of a single storey portico and pediments to the ground floor windows.   Demolished 1967.

MOYRIESK, Quin
A seven bay early to mid eighteenth-century house of two storeys with a three bay pedimented breakfront, and doorcase with lugged architrave. The main block was linked to single storey pavilions by quadrant walls with rusticated arched gateways. Home of the Rt. Hon. James FitzGerald M.P. at the end of the eighteenth century. The house was much altered in the late nineteenth century. Only a portion of the main block survives.

NEW GROVE HOUSE, Tulla
A plain, two storey, eighteenth-century house with a single storey porch. Seat of the Brown family.
Demolished. Walled garden and gates remain.

PARADISE HILL, Ennis
Two storey, bow fronted, gable-ended house, much altered in the late nineteenth century when the bows were given circular

high-pitched conical roofs. Former seat of the Henn family. Destroyed by fire 1970.

PARTEEN HOUSE, Parteen
Very attractive early nineteenth-century 'cottage'. Single storey gable-ended porch and Tudor chimney-stacks.
Demolished *c.*1926.

RAHEEN HOUSE, Tuamgraney
A two storey, early nineteenth-century, crenellated house. Seat of the Brady family.
Demolished. Walled garden, outbuildings and gate lodge survive.

RIVERSTOWN, Corofin
Plain, mid eighteenth-century, five bay, two storey, gable-ended house, the walls of which have a definite batter. Seat of James Lysaght in 1814.   Derelict.

SEAMOUNT, Liscannor   In ruins.

TIERMACLANE, Ennis
An early to mid eighteenth-century two storey house with Venetian doorcase. Seat of the Woulfe family.
In ruins since 1840.

TYREDAGH CASTLE, Tulla
A plain two storey house built in 1809 for Thomas Browne. Burnt *c.*1903.   Ruin demolished in 1956. New house on site.

WILLIAMSTOWN HOUSE, Williamstown
A two storey, early nineteenth-century, castellated house. Seat of the Gibson family. Burnt in the 1920's.   Demolished.

WOODPARK, Bunratty
Mid to late eighteenth-century house. Five bay, three storey, gable-ended, slate hung front with Venetian doorcase and Venetian windows on first and second storeys under a small pediment. Seat of the Daltons. In ruins before 1911. Demolished.

Facing page:
Birchfield: Entrance front.
Old photograph. Collection Hon. Mrs. Grania Weir.

Above:
Moyriesk: Entrance front.
Old photograph.

Right:
Woodpark: Entrance front c.1975.
Photograph: William Garner.

Castle Mary: Entrance front before late 19th century alterations.

COUNTY CORK

ANNEMOUNT, Glounthaune
A late eighteenth-century house remodelled by George Ashlin *c.* 1883 for John Murphy. Italianate campanile tower at one end. Burnt in 1948 and since demolished.

ANNGROVE, Carrigtwohill
A very important late seventeenth-century and early eighteenth-century, two storey house for Sir James Cotter M.P. Five bay with projecting square corner towers which had high-pitched pyramidal roofs.   Demolished.

ARDNAGASHEL, Glengarriff
In 1814 the seat of A. Hutchins.   Demolished.

ARDRUM, Inniscarra
Large Georgian house. Seat of the Colthurst family. Demolished.

ASHGROVE, Cobh
A plain late Georgian house designed by Abraham Hargrave for Councillor Franklin.   Now a ruin.

BALLINTOBER, Ballinhassig
Very important, mid to late seventeenth-century, two storey house built for Lt.-Col. William Meade. Seven bay entrance front between projecting gable-ended wings. High-pitched roof with dormer-windows.   Demolished in the 1940's.

BALLYCLOUGH, Kilworth
A large, two storey, gable-ended house with a Gothic Revival garden front of early nineteenth-century appearance. In 1814 the seat of Col. Barry.   Demolished.

BALLYEDMOND, Midleton
A large early eighteenth-century house altered in the late eighteenth century by Abraham Hargrave the elder and younger for Robert Courtenay.   Demolished in the 1960's.

BALLYGIBLIN, Mallow
Good Tudor Revival house designed *c.* 1836 by William Vitruvius Morrison for Sir William Wrixon Becher incorporating an earlier house. Still intact in 1960.   Now a ruin.

BALLYMAGOOLY HOUSE, Mallow
An attractive early to mid Georgian house. The seat of the Courtneys in 1814.
Demolished after a fire in 1956.

BELFORT, Charleville
A two storey, cement rendered, mid to late nineteenth-century house.   Demolished in 1958.

BELGROVE, Cobh
Plain, two storey, late Georgian house. The seat of J. Travers in 1814.   Demolished in 1954.

BOWEN'S COURT, Kildorrery
Built by Henry Bowen between 1766 and 1776 and attributed to Isaac Rothery. The somewhat old fashioned style of the exterior would suggest a date of *c.* 1730. The entrance hall had superb pedimented doorcases and mahogany doors (now in a private collection).
The house was sold by the late Elizabeth Bowen, the novelist, in 1959.
Demolished in 1961.

BRIDE PARK, Ovens
A two storey, mid to late eighteenth-century, gable-ended house. In 1814 the seat of Rev. Spread.
Now a ruin.

BRIGHTFIELDSTOWN, Minane Bridge
Mid to late eighteenth-century house with an early nineteenth-century doorcase. Spacious staircase lit by a Venetian window. Former seat of the Roberts family who sold it in 1853.
Demolished 1984.

BUTTEVANT CASTLE, Buttevant
An early nineteenth-century conversion for John Anderson of part of the fortification of the town of Buttevant into a private house.   Now a ruin.

BYBLOX, Doneraile
A large, plain, three storey, late eighteenth-century house. In 1814 the seat of John Crone.
Demolished.

CAHERMONE, Midleton
House demolished, but ruinous stables remain.

CARRIG, Killavullen
House demolished except for a ruined tower which was part of one wing. In 1814 the seat of W. Franks.

Above and right:
Hoddersfield: Entrance hall 1966, and front door.
Photographs: Hugh Doran.

Facing page, top left:
Monkstown Castle:
Photograph: William Garner 1986.

Top right:
Ballyclough.
Victorian photograph. Collection: Irish Architectural Archive.

Bottom:
Castle Bernard: Entrance front.
Photograph: Robert French, Lawrence Coll., Nat. Library of Ireland.

CARRIGMORE, Montenotte, Cork city
An attractive, early to mid nineteenth-century, pedimented, classical house with a central semi-circular Roman Ionic portico. Former seat of the Murphy family.   Derelict.

CASTLE BERNARD, Bandon
A large, two storey, classical house built in 1798 for Francis Bernard, 1st Viscount Bandon. Joined to a tower house by a single storey corridor. The house had a good interior which included an entrance hall with a screen of columns at one end, and a cantilevered stone staircase. Gothic tracery was inserted in the windows in the mid Victorian period. Destroyed by fire in 1921.   Now a ruin.

CASTLE COOKE, Kilworth
Late seventeenth-century or early eighteenth-century house extended at various times by the Cooke family who acquired it in the second half of the seventeenth century.
Destroyed by fire in 1921.

CASTLE COR, Kanturk
Important, early eighteenth-century, two storey house with a swan necked pedimented doorcase and a high-pitched roof with dormer-windows. The house was much extended in the early nineteenth century. Built for the Freemans. The doorcase and other stonework are now in a private collection.
Demolished c. 1965.

CASTLE FREKE, Rosscarbery
A large classical house built c. 1790 by Sir John Evans-Freke, altered by Richard Morrison c. 1820, when he also designed the large office court. The original house was at the same time remodelled in the Tudor Revival style. The main block was destroyed by fire in 1910. In the subsequent rebuilding Morrison's alterations were simplified. The house was stripped of its fittings in 1952.   Now a ruin.

CASTLE HARRISON, Charleville
Three storey, gable-ended, early eighteenth-century house incorporating an earlier castle. Seat of the Harrisons. Demolished c. 1960.

CASTLE MARY, Cloyne
An interesting, three storey, late seventeenth-century and early eighteenth-century house with a recessed three bay centre flanked by single bay projecting wings. The walls of these wings at ground floor level have a very distinct 'batter'. The pedimented doorcase was late eighteenth-century with engaged columns having 'Tower of the Winds' capitals. The architect Davis Duckart is recorded as having designed a 'difficult' roof for the house. The house was much altered in the late nineteenth century, in the 'baronial' style. A seat of the Longfields. It was destroyed by fire in 1920.
Now a ruin. A good stable court survives.

CONVAMORE, Ballyhooly
Very plain, early nineteenth-century, classical house designed by James Pain for the Earl of Listowel. Burnt in 1921.
Now a ruin.

CORKBEG, Whitegate
A two storey early nineteenth-century house. Very fine top-lit stone staircase with brass balusters. In 1814 the seat of Robert FitzGerald. Demolished to make way for Whitegate refinery.

Facing page:

Ballygiblin.
Old photograph c.1911. Copy photograph: David Davison.

Ballygiblin: In ruins. 1986.
Photograph: William Garner.

Above:

Garretstown: View from stable block c.1965.
Photograph: Lord Rossmore.

Top right:
Mount Uniacke:
Old photograph. Collection: Peter Lamb.

Bottom right:
Dromagh Castle.
Photograph: William Garner.

CURRAGLASS, Curraglass
A Georgian house and a seat of the Wallis family. Having stood for many years as a ruin, it has recently been demolished to make way for road improvements.

DERRY, Rosscarbery
A plain late Georgian house with flanking two storey single bay pavilions. A seat of the Townshends.
Burnt *c.* 1922.

DROMAGH CASTLE, Millstreet
House demolished, but a fine castellated stable block remains. The seat in 1814 of N.P. Leader.

DROMDIHY HOUSE, Killeagh
Classical house built for Roger Green Davis in 1833. Two storey, five bay central block flanked by single storey wings. The entrance is at one end under a superb and very correct Doric portico.   Now a ruin.

DUARRIGLE CASTLE, Millstreet
An early nineteenth-century castellated house. Former seat of the Justice family.   Now a ruin.

DUNBOY CASTLE, Castletownberehaven
Designed by John Christopher in 1866-1867 for H.L. Puxley and carried out by E.H. Carson of Dublin incorporating a tower house and a later house of 1838. The earlier house became the service wing. The chief glory of the house was the great hall, rising through three floors with the roof supported on granite transverse arches. The house was burnt in August, 1921. Now a ruin.

DUNSLAND, Glanmire, Cork city
A late Victorian gabled house.   Burnt *c.* 1920.

FERMOY HOUSE, Fermoy
A very attractive late eighteenth-century and early nineteenth-century classical house consisting of a five bay central block with a semi-circular Roman Doric portico flanked by single storey pedimented pavilions. The former seat of John Anderson. Demolished.

FLAXFORT, Little Island
A five bay, two storey, gable-ended house with a single storey Doric portico.   Derelict.

FORT ROBERT, Ballineen
A two storey weather slated house built in 1788 for R.L. Conner. A ruin by the end of the nineteenth century.

GARRETTSTOWN, Ballinspittle
Two early to mid eighteenth-century pavilions facing each other across a forecourt remain and it is not known for certain if the main block was in fact ever built. These pavilions each have five bay pedimented facades with central rusticated doorcases. One seems to have served as a house while the other served as a stable. Built for the Kearney family.   Now derelict.

GLENGARRIFF LODGE, Glengarriff
A very large early nineteenth-century cottage orné built by the 1st Earl of Bantry.   Demolished.

GLYNTOWN, Glanmire, Cork city
A late Georgian villa built for Samuel Micall. Demolished *c.* 1930's.

GORTIGRENANE, Minane Bridge
A three storey late eighteenth-century house joined to pavilions by arcaded screen walls, good interior plasterwork. A former seat of the Daunt family.   Derelict.

Facing, left:
Duarrigle Castle: Entrance front.
Photograph: Robert French, Lawrence Coll., Nat. Library of Ireland.

Facing, right:
Buttevant Castle: Old postcard view.
Gillman Collection.

Above:
Dunboy Castle:
Photograph: c.1890 by Robert French, Lawrence Coll., Nat. Library of
Ireland. Copy photograph: David Davison.

Right:
Palace Anne.

HODDERSFIELD, Crosshaven
A large, plain, late eighteenth-century or early nineteenth-century, three storey house designed by Abraham Hargrave the elder for W.H. Moore-Hodder. The entrance front was rendered over weather slating. Good cantilevered stone main staircase with very fine wrought iron balustrade.   Now a ruin.

INNISHANNON, Innishannon
A bow fronted, two storey, Georgian house.   Burnt in 1921.

KILBOY, Cloyne
A plain, two storey, late eighteenth-century and early nineteenth-century house. The seat of Lewis Gibson in 1814.
Now a ruin.

KILBYRNE, Doneraile
A two storey early nineteenth-century house with a single storey Roman Doric portico. The former seat of the Grove Whites. Demolished after 1956.

KILCOLEMAN, Bandon
A three storey, plain, late eighteenth-century house with a nineteenth-century porch on the entrance front.
Burnt in 1921.

LEAMLARA, Carrigtwohill
A two storey mid eighteenth-century house built for the Barry family, much altered in the early nineteenth century. Good staircase.   Demolished since 1956.

LITTLE ISLAND HOUSE, Little Island
A large late eighteenth-century house sometimes attributed to Davis Duckart because of the similarity of its plan to that of Kilshannig. Seven bay, three storey centre block with Doric pedimented doorcase, flanked by two storey pavilions linked to the entrance front by quadrant walls. Built for the Bury family. Now a ruin.

LOHORT CASTLE, Cecilstown
A large fifteenth-century tower house restored in the mid eighteenth century by the 2nd Earl of Egmont. The castle was remodelled in 1876 when the crow stepped gables, bawn wall and gatehouse were built.
The castle was destroyed by fire in 1920.

MACROOM CASTLE, Macroom
A fifteenth-century castle reconstructed in the early nineteenth century for Robert Hedges Eyres. Burnt in 1920.
Now a ruin.

MAYFIELD (formerly KNOCKANEMEELE), Bandon
A late seventeenth-century and early eighteenth-century house remodelled in the late eighteenth century. A porch was added in 1872. Seat of the Pooles.   Burnt in 1921.

MITCHELSTOWN CASTLE, Mitchelstown
Designed by James and George Richard Pain in 1823 for the 3rd Earl of Kingston. One of the largest early Gothic Revival castles in Ireland. Very fine interior which included a vaulted gallery. Destroyed by fire in 1922. The ruin was afterwards demolished and the cut stone used to build a new church at Mount Melleray Abbey, Co. Waterford.

MONKSTOWN CASTLE, Monkstown
An early seventeenth-century semi-fortified house built for Anastasia Archdekin which until recently was one of the few houses of this date in Ireland still roofed, another example being Rathfarnham Castle, Co. Dublin. The hall has a chimney-piece dated 1636. The house was restored in the late eighteenth century.   Now a ruin.

MOORE PARK, Kilworth
A three storey, plain, late Georgian house with flanking two storey wings which may be later. Former seat of the Earls of Mount Cashell.   Burnt in 1908.

MOUNT MASSY, Macroom
A seven bay two storey centre block was flanked by pedimented arches connected to the ends of the stables which have Venetian and Diocletian windows in the end elevation. The facades of the stable blocks which face each other across the yard have pedimented breakfronts. The foundation stone is dated 1783. In 1814 the seat of Hubert Baldwin.
Main block in ruins.

MOUNT UNIACKE, Killeagh
Important, early eighteenth-century, single storey house raised on a high basement built for the Uniacke family. Five bay entrance front with simple architrave doorcase. Steep sprocketed roof with dormer-windows. Late eighteenth-century bow window on side elevation.   Burnt in March 1923.

NEWBERRY MANOR, Mallow
A large, plain, three storey, late Georgian house.
Demolished.

NEW COURT, Skibbereen
A house dating from the Georgian period. In 1814 the seat of Beecher Fleming Esq.   Demolished.

OLD COURT, Doneraile
A two storey mid eighteenth-century house, much altered in the early nineteenth century. The seat of Joseph Stawell in 1814. Derelict.

PALACE ANNE, Ballineen
A very important and unique house built in 1714 for Arthur Bernard. Centre block of three storeys over a high basement with three curvilinear gables linked by one bay wings to two bay

pavilions also with curvilinear gables. The pedimented doorcase of the central block was mid eighteenth century. The house was faced with red brick, with cut stone dressings. Good interior with panelled rooms. Main block after standing as a ruin for many years was demolished in the late 1950's, only the left hand pavilion remains.

PEMBROKE, Passage West
Mid eighteenth-century three storey house. Five bay elevation with Venetian window on first floor above doorcase and Diocletian window above.   Demolished *c.*1975

PROSPECT VILLA, Ringaskiddy
Six bay, two storey, slate hung, late eighteenth-century house. Good broken pedimented doorcase.   Derelict 1975.

ROSTELLAN CASTLE, Rostellan
A large, mid eighteenth-century, three storey house enlarged in 1777 and again in the early nineteenth century when a Gothic porch and chapel wing were added. The house was probably built for the 4th Earl of Inchiquin.
Demolished 1944. A Doric column remains in the grounds.

RYE COURT, Farnanes
Plain eighteenth-century house with later entrance porch. Seat of the Rye family.   Burnt in 1921.

SAFFRON HILL, Doneraile
A very interesting early to mid eighteenth-century house. The house which is only single storey is built of a very beautiful brick. The doorcase is Venetian in form. The window sills are moulded. The house seems to have been originally thatched and the rooms were finished with very good classical cornices etc. Having stood derelict for many years, it was recently re-roofed, but is now derelict again. In 1814 the seat of Mrs. Brazier.

TIVOLI, Cork city
Large late eighteenth-century house built for James Morrison which consisted of centre block joined to pedimented pavilions by straight arcaded links. The house was damaged by fire in the 1820's and rebuilt, but was demolished in recent years.

TRABOLGAN, Whitegate
A two storey late Georgian house to which single storey bow fronted wings were added in the early nineteenth century. Single storey Doric entrance portico. Former seat of the Roche family, Lords Fermoy.   The house was recently demolished.

VELVETSTOWN, Buttevant
A large late nineteenth-century house built in 1875 for Christopher Crofts. The walls were built of yellow brick with red brick banding and limestone window cases. Destroyed by fire in 1895 and now a ruin.

WARRENSCOURT, Macroom
House demolished, but stable yard remains. In 1814 the seat of Sir Aug. Warren Bart.

Left:
Dromdihy House:
Photograph: William Garner 1986.

Right:
Castle Cor: Entrance front.

COUNTY DONEGAL

ARDS, Sheephaven
Two storey house built *c.*1830 to the design of John Hargrave of Cork for Alexander Stewart. Single storey pedimented Doric porch above which was a Venetian window. Demolished *c.*1965. Substantial U-shaped stables remain.

CAMLIN, Ballyshannon
Tudor Revival castle designed by John B. Keane in 1838 for John Tredenick incorporating an earlier house. The Gothic arched entrance gate remains.   Demolished.

CASTLE WRAY, Letterkenny   Demolished.

LOUGH ESKE CASTLE, Donegal
Large Elizabethan-style house designed by Fitzgibbon Louch and built between 1859-1861 for the Brookes, additions made 1914. Destroyed by fire 1939 except for one wing which is still occupied.

LOUGH VEAGH HOUSE, Gartan
Large picturesque villa designed by John Hargrave of Cork *c.*1825 for D. Chambers.   Demolished *c.*1970.

MALIN HALL, Clonca
A two storey early eighteenth-century house. The seat of Robert Harvey in 1814.   Burnt *c.*1920.

MEENGLAS, Stranorlar
Tudor Revival Victorian house.   Demolished 1948.

RAPHOE BISHOP'S PALACE, Raphoe
Built in 1661 by Bishop Robert Leslie and restored in the mid eighteenth century. Destroyed by fire in the late 1830's. Now a ruin.

SPRINGFIELD MANOR, Fanard
A two storey late seventeenth-century house. Partially demolished 1911-12, completely demolished 1968.

WARDSTOWN, Ballyshannon
A three storey house built in 1740 somewhat in the style of Sir John Vanburgh's smaller houses. Pair of staircases at the rere of the corner towers seem to be slightly later addition. Now a ruin.

Facing page:
Bishop's Palace, Raphoe: Front doorcase 1971.

Below:
Entrance front.
Photographs: William Garner.

Above:
Wardstown: Entrance front.
Photograph: Alistair Rowan.

Facing, top:
Lough Eske Castle.
Photograph: Alistair Rowan c.1969.

Facing, bottom:
Camlin: Entrance front c.1890.
Photograph: Robert French, Lawrence Collection, Nat. Library of Ireland.
Copy photograph: David Davison.

Killakee: Garden front c.1890.
Photograph: Robert French, Lawrence Coll., Nat. Library of Ireland.

COUNTY DUBLIN

ALLENTON, Tallaght
A very attractive, early to mid eighteenth-century, yellow washed house built for Sir Timothy Allen. Demolished in September 1984.

ASHTON HOUSE, Monkstown
Three storey mid to late eighteenth-century house with pedimented Doric doorcase. Re-roofed in the nineteenth century when a Doric porch was also added. The home of William Andrews in 1875. Demolished.

BALGRIFFIN PARK, Balgriffin
A two storey early eighteenth-century house with very fine segmental pedimented doorcase. Interior altered in early twentieth century. Derelict in 1965. Demolished.

BALLINCLEA, Killiney
A two storey bow fronted house built c.1830. Single storey granite portico. Seat of the Hon. Mrs. Mellifont in 1837. Demolished.

BRACKENSTOWN HOUSE (18th century house), Swords
A large, three storey, early to mid eighteenth-century house built for Robert 1st Viscount Molesworth, with a single storey Doric portico much altered in the nineteenth century. Destroyed by fire 1913. New house built on site to design of R.C. Orpen and P.L. Dickinson 1914.

BRAZEEL HOUSE, Swords
A three storey gabled house built in the 1630's. Its most important feature was the superb arcaded brick southern chimney-stack. A ruin for many years, it was demolished in 1976.

CASTLE BAGOT, Newcastle
A large, three storey, late eighteenth-century house. Good pedimented doorcase. Seat of Gerald Bagot in 1814. Now a ruin.

CLOVERHILL, Clondalkin
Two storey, bow fronted, late eighteenth-century house. In 1875 the home of Robert M'Intire. Now a ruin.

CORKAGH, Clondalkin
A large, three storey, early eighteenth-century house altered in the late eighteenth century when a single storey porch was added. Seat of the Finlays. Demolished in the 1960's.

CROYDON PARK, Marino
Large mid Georgian house much altered in the early nineteenth century. Demolished in the 1920's.

DAWSON COURT, Cross Avenue, Booterstown
A plain, three storey, late eighteenth-century house. Seat of James Mills in 1875. Demolished.

DELAFORD, Rathfarnham
A mid eighteenth-century house, originally an inn to which a new single storey front was added c.1800 by Alderman Bermingham. In the centre was the doorcase with its huge fanlight. This part of the house contained three rooms including the hall which could be linked to form one large room by means of large double doors. Demolished.

DELVILLE, Glasnevin
Charming, two storey, early eighteenth-century house with large mid eighteenth-century additions. Very fine interior with papier mâché rococo ceilings. Good chimney-pieces in main rooms. Some rooms had shell decoration by Mrs. Delany whose home it was. Demolished in the 1950's. One chimney-piece from the house survives in the hospital on its site, others were sold at the time of demolition.

DONAHIES (THE, formerly NEWBROOK HOUSE), Raheny
A very pleasant, two storey, late eighteenth-century house built of a beautiful brick. Demolished 1969.

ESKER, Lucan
Two storey mid eighteenth-century house with late eighteenth-century wings, with three sided bows. The seat of William F. Clarke in 1875. Demolished c.1977.

FARNHAM HOUSE, Finglas
A two storey, pedimented, late Georgian house with a single storey Doric portico. Demolished.

FORTFIELD, Terenure
Very fine, three storey, cut stone house built c.1785 for Chief Baron Yelverton, afterwards 1st Viscount Avonmore. Entrance front with single storey Doric portico. Good interior. Demolished 1940's.

FRASCATI, Blackrock
A mid eighteenth-century house, much altered and enlarged in the 1770's to the design of Thomas Owen for Emily, Duchess

of Leinster. Very fine interior which included a Portland stone main staircase, a drawing-room with a ceiling painted by Thomas Riley and chimney-pieces imported from France. The house was later divided into three.

The wings were demolished in 1981 and the remainder of the house in 1983.

GERALDINE HOUSE, Milltown

Interesting, two storey, pedimented, early eighteenth-century house. Rere elevation gabled, much altered in the nineteenth century, but some original interiors remained. In 1875 the home of Miss Troy.   Demolished recently.

GLENAGEARY HALL, Glenageary

A two storey early nineteenth-century house altered in the mid nineteenth century. In 1875 the home of Edward Fox J.P. Good interior plasterwork.   Demolished 1979.

GLENAGEARY HOUSE, Glenageary

A two storey early nineteenth-century house much altered possibly to the design of Sandham Symes. Sold to Thomas Pym in 1857.   Demolished 1979.

GRANITE HALL, Dun Laoghaire

A two storey, bow fronted, granite faced house built in 1821 by George Smith.   Demolished in the 1950's.

GROSVENOR HOUSE, Monkstown

A two storey late Victorian house with a mansard roof. Demolished.

GROVE HOUSE, Milltown

Fine mid eighteenth-century house much altered in the early to mid nineteenth century. Good drawing-room with coved ceiling. Demolished. This ceiling and other fittings were saved.

JOHNSTOWN KENNEDY, Rathcoole

A plain three storey house built in 1758 for Edward Kennedy, much altered and added to c.1830-1840. Very fine rococo ceilings in drawing-room and staircase.   Derelict.

KENURE PARK, Rush

A large early to mid eighteenth-century house altered c.1770 when the two large bowed drawing-rooms were created. These rooms had magnificent rococo ceilings and carved doorcases, that on the ground floor having a superb Doric chimney-piece. The house was altered and enlarged again in 1842 for Sir Roger Palmer Bart, to the design of George Papworth. Papworth refaced the house and added the granite Corinthian portico. He also created the entrance hall, the library and the central top-lit

staircase hall. The house was sold in 1964 and became derelict before its demolition in 1978. Samples of the rococo ceilings were saved by the Office of Public Works. Only the portico remains.

KILLAKEE, Rathfarnham

A large, two storey, early nineteenth-century house with single storey granite portico. Attractive interior included one room with Chinese wallpaper. Former seat of the Massys.   Demolished.

KILLESTER HOUSE, Killester

An outstanding, early eighteenth-century, single storey house. High-pitched roof with dormer-windows and a central pediment. Entrance front with recessed centre between projecting wings with Venetian windows. Seat of Sir William Newcomen in the late eighteenth century. Demolished c.1910. A chimneypiece and Venetian window surround from the house were used by Sir Edwin Lutyens at Howth Castle. A new house was built at Killester to the design of Frederick Hicks. This too has been demolished.

KILTERAGH, Foxrock

A large gabled house built 1905-1907 for Sir Horace Plunkett to the design of William D. Caroe. Burnt in 1923. Partly rebuilt.

KNOCKRABO, Kilmacud

Originally a small, two storey, early nineteenth-century villa. Extended in the mid nineteenth century when a single storey Roman Ionic portico was added.   Demolished.

LAKELANDS, Sandymount

A two storey late eighteenth-century house with early nineteenth-century wide eaved roof. Good doorcase.

Demolished c.1980. Doorcase re-erected at Ballymaloe, Co. Cork.

LISLE HOUSE, Crumlin

A very attractive, two storey, pedimented, early eighteenth-century brick house built for 1st Lord Lisle.   Demolished.

MANTUA, Swords

A three storey, bow ended, mid eighteenth-century house with single storey twentieth-century porch, similar to nearby Lissen Hall. In 1783 the seat of Mr. Keane.   Demolished.

Facing page:
Top: *Kenure Park: Entrance front c.1960.*
Bottom left: *Staircase.*
Photograph: National Parks & Monuments Branch, Commrs. of Public Works.
Bottom right: *Drawing room ceiling c.1960.*
Photograph: Lord Rossmore.

Above:
Turvey: Entrance front c.1950.

Right:
Newlands: Entrance front.
Old photograph.

Facing page:
Top: *St. Anne's: Entrance front with garden party 1912.*
Gillman Collection. Copy photograph: David Davison.

Bottom left: *Santry Court: Entrance front.*
Photograph: Gillman Collection.

Bottom right: *Mantua.*
Photograph: Maurice Craig.

MARETIMO, Blackrock
Plain mid Georgian house with good plasterwork built for Nicholas Lawless. Exterior much altered in the nineteenth century.   Demolished.

MARINO HOUSE, Clontarf
Mid eighteenth-century three storey house enlarged and improved after 1755 to the design of Sir William Chambers for James Caulfeild, 1st Earl of Charlemont. The house was further altered in the mid nineteenth century.   Demolished 1921.

MESPIL HOUSE, Mespil Road, Dublin
Originally a two storey villa with flanking single storey wings and a single storey entrance portico. The house was built in 1751 for Dr. Edward Barry, and was much altered later in the eighteenth century. The house had superb plasterwork, with three of the most important ceilings in Ireland.
The house was demolished c.1954 and the ceilings were transferred to Dublin Castle and Arás an Uachtaráin.

MILLTOWN HOUSE, Peamount
Plain, two storey, late eighteenth-century house, with later roof. In 1875 the seat of R.W. Boyle.   Derelict.

MILVERTON HALL, Skerries
Large, late nineteenth-century, cut stone, two storey house with mansard roof, single storey Doric portico. Seat of the Woods family.   Demolished in the 1960's.

MOUNT MERRION HOUSE, Stillorgan Rd., Dublin
Originally a three bay, two storey, early nineteenth-century house to which gable-ended wings were added. Very attractive, single storey, granite, Ionic porch.   Demolished c.1986.

MOUNTPELIER HOUSE, alias DOLLYMOUNT
A two storey, pedimented, bow fronted, late eighteenth-century house linked to tower like pavilions by screen walls.
Now a ruin.

NEWBURY HOUSE, Raheny
A two storey bow fronted house wih a good doorcase. Demolished.

NEWGROVE HOUSE, Balgriffin
An attractive, two storey, late eighteenth-century house. Good doorcase, oval drawing-room. Derelict in 1970.
Since demolished.

NEWLANDS, Clondalkin
Very fine, two storey, early eighteenth-century house much altered in the late eighteenth century and again in the early nineteenth century when the single storey Ionic portico was

Left: *White Hall: Drawing room ceiling 1979.*
Photograph: David Davison.

Right: *Johnstown Kennedy: Drawing room, ceiling detail 1986.*
Photograph: William Garner.

added. Very fine library and ball-room. The seat of the Wolfe family.   Recently demolished.

NUTGROVE, Rathfarnham

A two storey, pedimented, mid eighteenth-century house. A single storey portico was added in the present century. Very fine rococo plasterwork in interior, good staircases and chimney-pieces. Used as a boarding school in 1875.   Demolished.

OLD BAWN, Tallaght

Built *c.*1635 for William Buckeley, Archdeacon of Dublin. An important, two storey, gabled, 'H' plan house. The house was altered in the early eighteenth century when the Doric pedimented doorcase was added. Very fine interior with good seventeenth-century staircase and chimney-piece (both of which are now in the National Museum). The last remains of the house were demolished about ten years ago.

PAPAL NUNCIATURE, Phoenix Park

Former Under-Secretary's Lodge, originally a two storey mid Georgian villa incorporating a tower house. Much altered in the mid nineteenth century to the design of Jacob Owen. Recently demolished except for tower house and stables.

RAHENY PARK, Howth Rd., Raheny

A good quality, two storey, red brick villa built *c.*1790. Superb first floor drawing-room with coved ceiling. Demolished in the 1960's.

ROEBUCK GROVE, Clonskeagh

Plain, three storey, late eighteenth-century house with good doorcase and interior plasterwork. In 1875 the home of Robert Brewster.   Demolished *c.*1980.

ROSEMOUNT, Clonskeagh

A two storey late eighteenth-century villa, much extended in the early nineteenth century. Single storey porch added in the mid nineteenth century. The seat of John Corballis in 1875. Recently demolished.

ST. ANNE'S, Clontarf

Large, Italianate, two storey house built in 1880, for Arthur, 1st Lord Ardilaun to the design of James Franklin Fuller, incorporating an earlier house. Rich interior; entrance hall with Roman Ionic columns leading to a vast top-lit inner hall, with a gallery supported on Roman Ionic columns. To the right was the imperial main staircase in marble and on the left a palm court. The house was further enlarged to the design of George Ashlin who also designed the stables. The house was bought by Dublin Corporation in 1939 and badly damaged by fire in 1943. It stood derelict for twenty five years and was demolished in 1968. The grounds are now a public park.

Left: *Grove House: Drawing room 1974.*
Photograph: David Davison.

Right: *Nutgrove: First floor ceiling.*
Photograph: William Garner.

Above:
Delville: Mrs. Delany's boudoir, c.1950.
Photograph: Phyllis Thompson. Copy photograph: David Davison.

Top right:
Allenton: Entrance front.

Bottom right:
Old Bawn: Entrance front c.1900.
Photograph: Collection RSAI. Copy print: Richard Dann.

ST. GRELLANS, Monkstown Rd.
Very interesting Greek Revival villa built *c.*1840. Very severe single storey portico. Good interior.   Demolished *c.*1979.

SALMON POOL, Island Bridge
A two storey late nineteenth-century house.   Demolished.

SANS SOUCI, Booterstown
A mid to late eighteenth-century house altered and extended in 1802 for William Digges La Touche, to the design of Richard Morrison. Very fine interior with plasterwork by James Talbot. Demolished in the 1940's.

SANTRY COURT, Santry
An important early eighteenth-century house built *c.*1703 for 3rd Lord Barry of Santry. Wings were added in the mid eighteenth century. The house was much altered during the nineteenth century so that it is almost impossible to know what is genuine eighteenth-century work. The house was destroyed by fire in the 1940's and has since been demolished. The fine entrance doorcase is held in store by the Office of Public Works.

SCRIBBLESTOWN HOUSE, Finglas
A three storey Georgian house.   Destroyed by fire in 1976.

SOUTH HILL, Milltown
A bow fronted Georgian house.   Demolished *c.*1939.

STILLORGAN HOUSE, Stillorgan
A two storey late seventeenth-century house with flanking single storey wings, begun in 1695 for John Allen M.P. Sir Edward Lovett Pearce prepared plans for alterations and additions which were not carried out.   Demolished 1860.

THE PRIORY, Rathfarnham
Two storey Georgian house bought by John Philpot Curran in 1790.   Demolished in the 1940's.

THE TURRET, Glasnevin
Very interesting early eighteenth-century house with tower like centre block of two storeys flanked by single storey wings. Simple architrave doorcase. Much altered and extended in the late nineteenth century.   Demolished January 1986.

TRIMLESTOWN HOUSE, Merrion Rd., Dublin
Early nineteenth-century house, much altered and having a single storey Doric porch.   Demolished.

TURVEY, Donabate
Very important house of many periods. Basically a seventeenth-century house incorporating an earlier castle or tower house. The entrance front seems to have been on the east side. In the early eighteenth century a wing was added at right angles to this and the entrance was changed to the south. This front had a superb doorcase (similar to that at 33, Molesworth Street, now removed) with Ionic columns supporting a segmental pediment with urns and a coat of arms. The top floor then consisted of three gables with a Diocletian window in each. The house was again altered in the late eighteenth century when the space between the gables was filled in and the house was re-roofed. Very interesting interior with rooms of all periods. Late eighteenth-century hall and staircase, with mid eighteenth-century library. One ground floor room had a ceiling with rococo decoration in papier mâché. Seat of the Barnewall family.   Demolished in 1987.

WESTOWN HOUSE, The Naul
Large, two storey, early eighteenth-century house with single storey portico incorporating a tower house. Seat of the Hussey family.   Now a ruin.

WHITE HALL, Finglas Rd., Dublin
Very fine, two storey, mid Georgian house. Good interior with rococo plasterwork in drawing-room, fine open-well staircase and with pedimented doorcases.   Recently demolished.

WILLBROOK, Ranelagh Rd., Dublin
An important pedimented villa built *c.*1740. Much altered in the late eighteenth and early nineteenth centuries when the house became a convent. Good interior with panelled hall. Demolished in 1981.

WOODVILLE, Lucan
An attractive two storey villa attributed to Nathaniel Clements. The main block was joined to flanking pavilions by quadrant screen walls. Much altered in the nineteenth century. The home of Major General H.S. Scott in 1837. Demolished in the 1960's.

Portumna Castle: 19th century castle, c.1890.
Photograph: Robert French, Lawrence Coll., Nat. Library of Ireland.

COUNTY GALWAY

ARDFRY, Oranmore
A large, two storey, late eighteenth-century house altered in 1826 when it was probably given its battlements and Gothic doorcase. Seat of the Blake family.   Now a ruin.

ATHENRY HOUSE, Athenry
Simple late eighteenth-century house.   Demolished.

BALLYDONELAN CASTLE, Loughrea
A two storey late seventeenth-century house incorporating a tower house at one end. The seat of the Donelans. Much altered in the eighteenth century.   Now a ruin.

BEECHILL, New Inn
Mid to late eighteenth-century two storey house. Derelict in 1980.

BELVILLE, Athenry
Late eighteenth-century and early nineteenth-century classical house with three storey flanking crenellated tower which may be a later addition. In 1814 the seat of Richard Mack. Now a ruin.

BROOK LODGE, Tuam
A curious, late eighteenth-century and early nineteenth-century, bow fronted, two storey house.   Now a ruin.

BROWNES GROVE, Ballyconneely
An early nineteenth-century, three storey, slate hung house. Now a ruin.

BUNOWEN CASTLE, Clifden
A large late eighteenth-century and early nineteenth-century castle.   Now a ruin.

CASTLE DALY, Loughrea
An important three storey, seven bay, early to mid eighteenth-century house with a pedimented breakfront incorporating a tower house. Rere facade has battlements added in the early to mid nineteenth century. Built by the Dalys. Now a ruin. Only the rere elevation remains.

CASTLEGROVE, Tuam
A large, early nineteenth-century, two storey house with a single storey Roman Ionic portico. Seat of the Blakes. Burnt 1922.

CASTLEMOYLE, Tuam
Plain, late eighteenth-century, three storey house.   Now a ruin.

CASTLE TAYLOR, Ardrahan
An early nineteenth-century house built by the Taylors incorporating a superb tower house.   Now a ruin.

CASTLETOWN, Tuam
A two storey, gable-ended, late eighteenth-century and early nineteenth-century house built for the O'Haras.   Now a ruin.

CLIFDEN CASTLE, Clifden
Picturesque Norman Revival castle built *c.* 1815 for John D'Arcy. Now a ruin.

CLONBROCK, Ahascragh
Designed by William Leeson for Robert Dillon afterwards Lord Clonbrock and built 1780-1788. The hall and staircase had plasterwork in the style of Michael Stapleton. The main staircase of Portland stone had an elegant wrought iron balustrade. A single storey Doric portico was added to the entrance front *c.* 1824 and a new drawing-room wing in 1855. The house was sold in 1976 and destroyed by fire in 1984.   Now a ruin.

CLONFERT PALACE, Eyrecourt
Important, seventeenth-century, two storey house altered in the late eighteenth century. Damaged by fire in 1954 and now derelict.

COOLE, Gort
A very plain, three storey, late eighteenth-century house built for Robert Gregory to which a porch was added in the nineteenth century. The house as built was in complete contrast to the superb neo-classical house designed by James Lewis (*c.* 1751-1820) and published by him in his *Original designs in Architecture*, II, 1797.   Demolished 1941.

CROSS HOUSE, Menlough
Interesting, small, early nineteenth-century house consisting of a two storey, three sided, bay fronted centre, flanked by single storey wings.   Derelict.

DALYSTON, Loughrea
Important, mid eighteenth-century, cut stone, three storey house built for the Dalys. Pedimented Tuscan doorcase. The main

Facing:
Clonbrock: Main staircase, plasterwork.
Photograph: William Garner c.1975.

Above:
Eyrecourt: Entrance front c.1890.
Copy photograph: David Davison.

Right:
The main staircase from the entrance hall.

elevation is almost identical to Ballynahown Court, Co. Westmeath which dates from 1746. Dalyston was stripped in 1961 and is now a ruin.

DANESFIELD HOUSE, Moycullen
The seat of George Edmund Burke in 1875.   Demolished.

DUNSANDLE, Athenry
A very large and important mid to late eighteenth-century house built for Denis Daly M.P. The architect remains unknown. Very fine interior, saloon with doorcases and plasterwork which was identical to that in a room at Charlemont House, Dublin. Other interiors had neo-classical plasterwork for which drawings survive from the office of James Wyatt. The house was sold in 1954 and dismantled in 1958. Some ruins remain. The destruction of this house was a major loss to Ireland's architectural heritage and was all the more tragic because it was so recent.

EYRECOURT CASTLE, Eyrecourt
Important house built in the 1660's. The only other house of this type and date to survive is Beaulieu, Co. Louth. Seven bay, pedimented entrance front, the windows of which were reglazed in the late eighteenth-century or early nineteenth-century with Gothic sashes; superb doorcase, massive oak modillion cornice and high-pitched sprocketed roof with dormer-windows. Fine interior of which the chief glory was the magnificent carved oak staircase (now in store at the Detroit Institute of Arts). Now a ruin.

EYREVILLE, Kiltormer
A late eighteenth-century and early nineteenth-century house built for the Eyres.   Now a ruin.

HAMPSTEAD, Mount Bellew
A mid to late eighteenth-century, three storey, cut stone, bow fronted house.   Now a ruin.

KILLAGH, Kilconnell
A three storey mid to late eighteenth-century house with a Venetian window on the first floor above a pedimented tripartite doorcase (now removed). The house is now a ruin.

KILTULLAGH, Athenry
An important, late seventeenth-century and early eighteenth-century, two storey house. The very high chimney-stacks have sunk panels, and there are pistol-loops in the basement which is most unusual for a house of this period. This house which is now a ruin is a most impressive example of an early virtually undefended house and should be preserved from further depredation.

Bottom left:
Ardfry: Entrance front c.1870.
Copy photograph: David Davison.
Bottom right:
Ballydonelan Castle: Entrance front.
Collection: Mr Bertie Donohoe.

Facing page:
Top: *Castle Daly: Garden front c.1880.*
Photograph: Collection Bertie Donohoe. Copy photograph: David Davison.
Bottom left: *Castle Daly: Entrance front.*
Photograph: Collection Miss Olive Daly.
Facing, right: *Browne's Grove: Entrance front.*
Photograph: William Garner.

KNOCKBANE, Moycullen

An early nineteenth-century two storey house with Tudor Revival gables. Derelict by *c.*1880.

LISREAGHAN (also known as BELLEVUE), Lawrencetown

A very large two storey eighteenth-century house with a pedimented two storey Doric frontispiece, built for Walter Lawrence. The principal rooms of its lavish interior were the Aurora Hall, Constantine Hall and Italian drawing room, some of which were decorated with large frescoes. There was a sale of contents in 1912 and a final sale in the 1920's. The house was later demolished to provide building materials. A number of follies survive including a triumphal arch.

MARBLE HILL, Loughrea

A large, plain, three storey house built 1775 for John Burke. A large wing was added *c.*1813. Now a ruin.

MASONBROOK, Loughrea

An attractive and well designed, early nineteenth-century, cut stone house. Entrance front with single storey Greek Doric portico. Built for the Smyths. Now a ruin.

MENLOUGH CASTLE, Galway

A gabled tower house to which various additions have been made starting in the early eighteenth century. Seat of the Blake family. The castle was destroyed by fire in 1910 and is now a ruin.

MERLIN PARK, Galway

A large plain house built *c.*1808 for Charles Blake. The windows were altered to mullion and transom type later in the century. Demolished.

Below:
Clifton Castle: Entrance front c.1865.
Photograph: F.H. Mares.

Facing: *Dunsandle.*
Top left: *Saloon c.1890.*
Photograph: Collection Bowes Daly.
Top right: *Saloon plasterwork c.1975.*
Photograph: William Garner.
Bottom: *Entrance front c.1950.*

MONIVEA CASTLE, Athenry

An unusual early eighteenth-century house incorporating a tower house at the rere built by Patrick Ffrench. Single storey wings, to which an extra storey was added in the mid to late nineteenth century, flank a two storey pedimented centre block. Eighteenth-century house demolished and only the tower house survives.

MOUNT BELLEW, Mount Bellew Bridge

A late eighteenth-century, three storey, cut stone house to which pedimented wings and a single storey Roman Ionic portico were added *c.* 1820 to the design of Richard Morrison for C.D. Bellew. Morrison also remodelled the original house. Superb interior. Demolished.

MOUNT BERNARD, Mount Bellew

A very attractive early nineteenth-century three bay, two storey villa, in the style of Richard Morrison. In 1844 the seat of B. Brown.   Demolished.

MOUNT HAZEL, Ballymacward

A three storey late eighteenth-century and early nineteenth-century house built for the Browne family.   Demolished 1945.

MOYODE CASTLE, Athenry

A large early nineteenth-century castle built by the Persse family. Now a ruin.

Below:
Mount Bellew: Entrance front c. 1885.
Collection: Mrs. Grattan-Bellew.

Facing page:
Top: *Mount Bellew: Library 1885.*
Collection: Mrs. Grattan-Bellew.

Bottom left: *Mount Bellew: Dining room 1885.*
Collection: Mrs. Grattan-Bellew.

Bottom right: *Lisreaghan: Entrance front.*
Photograph: Collection Fr. Egan.

NETTERVILLE LODGE, Mount Bellew
A two storey early to mid nineteenth-century house with a single storey portico with 'Tower of the Winds' capitals.
Demolished.

PALLAS, Loughrea
A three storey late eighteenth-century house designed by William Leeson for Anthony Nugent, Lord Riverston. Much altered in the nineteenth century.
Demolished.

PORTUMNA CASTLE (19th Century castle), Portumna
Ruskinian Gothic mansion designed by Sir Thomas Newenham Deane in 1862 for the 1st Marquess of Clanricarde.
Destroyed by fire 1922.

RAHASANE PARK, Loughrea
Very fine early nineteenth-century villa in the style of Richard Morrison. The seat of Robert Trench in 1814.
Demolished, gate lodge remains.

RAMORE, Ballinasloe
A large eighteenth-century house unusual in that it consists of a three bay three storey centre between two three sided bays which are only two storeys but of the same overall height.
Demolished.

ROOKWOOD, Ballygar
A three storey mid to late eighteenth-century house to which a single storey Ionic portico was added in the early nineteenth century. The seat of the Thewles family.   Demolished c.1950.

Clonbrock: Entrance front.

ROSSHILL LODGE, Clonbur
House demolished but stables remain, converted into a house.

ROXBOROUGH, Loughrea
An early to mid eighteenth-century gable-ended house with later additions. The seat of the Persse family.
Burnt 1922, some ruins remain.

RYEHILL, Athenry
A large, two storey, late Georgian house. The seat of the Redingtons.   Demolished.

SOMERSET HOUSE, Ballinasloe
A three storey late Georgian house.   Demolished.

SPRINGFIELD, Williamstown
A very attractive, early to mid eighteenth-century, two storey, thatched house.   Demolished.

TYRONE HOUSE, Clarinbridge
A large, cut stone, three storey house built in 1779 to the design of John Roberts of Waterford for Christopher St. George. Similar in many details to Moore Hall Co. Mayo. Very fine plasterwork in main rooms. The house was burnt in 1920 and the ruin is now in the care of the Irish Georgian Society.

WESTON, Ahascragh
An important, early nineteenth-century, two storey villa designed by Richard Morrison for the Mahon family. Similar to the same architect's Cangort Park and Bellair both in Co. Offaly. All three feature an entrance door set in a deep tunnel-like arched recess.
Demolished.

Facing page, left to right:
Menlough Castle.
Photograph 1896.

Dalyston: Front doorcase c.1970.
Photograph: David Davison.

Moyode Castle: Entrance front.
Collection: Mr Bertie Donohoe.

Weston: Entrance front.
Old photograph.

Rahasane Park: Entrance front c.1870.

Rookwood.
Old photograph.

Above:
Kenmare House (also known as Killarney House):
East front.
Old photograph. Copy photograph: William Garner.

Facing page:
Glenflesk Castle: Entrance front.
Old photograph.

COUNTY KERRY

ARDFERT ABBEY, Ardfert
An important late seventeenth-century house altered in the early eighteenth century for Maurice Crosbie. Two storey main block with pedimented centre flanked by two bay projections. High-pitched roof on a stone modillion cornice. Panelled hall decorated with painted figures. Superb carved and panelled staircase. Further alterations were carried out *c.* 1830.
Demolished.

ARDTULLY, Kenmare
A large, early Victorian, baronial house, built for Sir Richard Orpen. Burnt in 1921. Now a ruin.

BALLYCARTY, Tralee
Plain house.   Now a ruin.

BALLYHEIGUE CASTLE, Tralee
A large Tudor Revival house designed by Richard and William Vitruvius Morrison for James Crosbie *c.* 1809, incorporating an earlier house. The house was burnt in 1921, and one wing was recently restored.

CARHAN, Cahirciveen
A ruin since the early nineteenth century.

CASTLEQUIN, Cahirciveen
A mid nineteenth-century gabled house. Seat of the Mahony family.   Derelict.

CROTTO, Kilflynn
A seventeenth-century house altered by Richard Morrison *c.* 1819 for the Carrique-Ponsonby family.   Demolished.

DERRYQUIN CASTLE, Sneem
A medium sized Victorian castle designed by James Franklin Fuller for the Bland family.   Burnt in 1922.

DICK'S GROVE, Currow
In 1928 the seat of R.S.W. Meredith. Demolished. Stables survive.

GLENBEIGH TOWERS, Glenbeigh
An important house designed by Edward William Godwin in the form of a late medieval tower house and built between 1867 and 1871 for Hon. Rowland Winn. Burnt in 1922. Parts of the ruin still survive.

GLENFLESK CASTLE Killarney
(also known as FLESK CASTLE)
An early nineteenth-century castellated house built for John Coltsmann.   Now a magnificent hill top ruin.

KENMARE HOUSE, Killarney
(also known as KILLARNEY HOUSE)
A large, red brick, Tudor style mansion designed by George Devey c.1877 for the 4th Earl of Kenmare and carried out by William Henry Lynn. It replaced a house built in 1726. Destroyed by fire in 1913. Ruin demolished c.1956.

KILCOLEMAN ABBEY Milltown
(formerly MILLTOWN HOUSE)
A plain three storey house built c.1800, altered in the Tudor Revival style by Richard and William Vitruvius Morrison in 1819 for Sir John Godfrey. Abandoned c.1960, some ruins remain.

KILMORNA, Listowel
A gabled Victorian house. Seat of the Mahony family. Burnt in 1921.

LIXNAW, Lixnaw
An old castle enlarged in the eighteenth century. The former seat of the FitzMaurices, Earls of Kerry. In ruins by 1837, little remains.

SALLOW GLEN, Tarbert
A plain, early to late eighteenth-century, three storey, gable-ended house. A large two storey wing was added to the rere in the late eighteenth century. In 1814 the seat of Thomas Sands. House demolished but parts of the stables remain.

SANDFORD HOUSE
A two storey, eighteenth-century, gable-ended house. In 1814 the seat of Nicholas Neilan. Demolished.

Facing page:
Ardfert Abbey: Entrance front.
Photograph c.1870. Collection: Col. Talbot Crosbie.

Above:
Ardfert Abbey: Drawing room.
Old photograph.

Right:
Glenbeigh Towers.
Photograph by Robert French c.1890. Lawrence Coll., Nat. Library of Ireland.

COUNTY KILDARE

ARDRASS HOUSE, Celbridge
A two storey, pedimented, early eighteenth-century house, altered *c.*1750.   Demolished.

BELAN, Ballitore
A large, three storey, gable-ended house designed by Richard Castle and Francis Bindon. Abandoned in the mid nineteenth century. The ruins have been demolished. Superb stables and follies remain.

DONADEA CASTLE, Prosperous
A large seventeenth-century (and earlier) castle much altered *c.*1800 to the design of Richard Morrison for the Aylmer family. Now a ruin.

Facing page:
Donadea Castle: Entrance front c.1975.
Photograph: William Garner.

DONORE HOUSE, Prosperous
Good, late eighteenth-century, brick house, pedimented Ionic doorcase.   Now a ruin.

HODGESTOWN, Timahoe
Ruined remains of very interesting early eighteenth-century house.

HORTLAND, Kilcock
A two storey house built in 1748 for the Rt. Rev. Josiah Hort Archbishop of Tuam and attributed to Richard Castle. Demolished.

KILMORONY, Athy
A two storey late Georgian house. In 1814 the seat of Peter Bell. Demolished.

LEIXLIP HOUSE, Leixlip
A very attractive early to mid eighteenth-century house. Good interior. A bow fronted wing was added in the early nineteenth century.   Recently destroyed by fire. Now a ruin.

Below:
Hortland: Entrance front.
Photograph c.1913.

LONGTOWN, Clane

A large, plain, early eighteenth-century house much enlarged later in the century by Captain George Burdett. Early nineteenth-century Ionic portico.　Demolished.

MORRISTOWN LATTIN, Naas

A late seventeenth-century house built by the Lattin family, remodelled in the Tudor Revival style for G.P.L. Mansfield in 1845 to the design of William Deane Butler.
Recently badly damaged by fire.

NEWPARK, Kilmeage

A late eighteenth-century house now in ruins. Doorcase capitals now at Robertstown presbytery. The seat of Rev. Hannesly in 1814.

RATHANGAN HOUSE, Rathangan

A plain late eighteenth-century house.　Demolished.

RATHCOFFEY, Maynooth

An interesting, early to mid eighteenth-century, three storey house incorporating an earlier building. Sold in the 1780's by the 2nd Lord Talbot de Malahide to Archibald Hamilton Rowan. The ground floor is vaulted.
Now a ruin.

SALLYMOUNT, Brannockstown

A large, plain, late eighteenth-century house with Victorian additions built by the Cramer Roberts family.
Demolished.

Facing page:
Morristown Lattin: Garden front.
Photograph c.1900. Gillman Collection.

Above:
Rathcoffey: Entrance front c.1975.
Photograph: William Garner.

COUNTY KILKENNY

BELLEVUE HOUSE, Slieverue
A three storey late Georgian house with a good Doric doorcase. A strange, two storey, canted portico was added in the late nineteenth century by the Power family.
Dismantled *c*.1940. The ruin has since collapsed.

CASTLECOMER HOUSE, Castlecomer
A very large eighteenth-century house with nineteenth-century additions. Battlemented parapet.
Burnt in 1965 and now largely demolished.

CASTLE MORRES, Kilmaganny
A large mid eighteenth-century house designed by Francis Bindon for the Morres family. Very fine interior with good plasterwork. Altered in the early nineteenth century by Daniel Robertson of Kilkenny. Partially demolished following a demolition sale in 1940. Ruin recently demolished.

CHAPELIZOD HOUSE, Kells
House dated 1672 and 1748. Unusual ground plan and some remains of mid eighteenth-century plasterwork. In ruins.

DANES FORT, Danesfort
A late seventeenth-century and early eighteenth-century house with later alterations. In 1814 the seat of James Wemys. Demolished.

Facing page:
Castle Morres: Entrance hall chimneypiece c.1912.
Photograph: G.D. Croker.
Below: *Entrance front c.1900.*
Photograph: Collection Mrs. de Montmorency.

DESART COURT, Callan

A superb house built in 1733 for John Cuffe, 1st Lord Desart. The general design of the house was inspired by the Queen's House Greenwich designed by Inigo Jones. Desart may have been designed by Sir Edward Lovett Pearce as its plan was similar to his Bishop's Palace at Cashel. Very fine interior with good plasterwork and joinery. The house was burnt in 1923 but well restored by the architect Richard Orpen. A demolition sale was held in 1943. The ruins were demolished *c.*1957. The destruction of this house was one of Ireland's greatest architectural losses.

FLOOD HALL, Thomastown

A two storey late eighteenth-century house altered in the early nineteenth century and again in the late nineteenth century. Seat of the Flood family.   Demolished in 1950.

FOYLE HOUSE, Balleen

A small, two storey, late Georgian house.   Now a ruin.

GLASHARE HOUSE, Coolnacutta

A two storey, early nineteenth-century, gable-ended house. Demolished.

JENKINSTOWN, Ballyragget

An early, nineteenth-century, Gothic house designed by William Robertson built for Major George Bryan. The centre block was demolished later in the nineteenth century and not rebuilt. Now mostly demolished.

KELLYMOUNT

A two storey early eighteenth-century house altered in the early nineteenth century.   Derelict.

Facing page: *Castle Morres:*
Entrance hall, plasterwork above chimneypiece in decay, 1977.
Photograph: William Garner.

Below: *Desart Court: Entrance front c.1915.*
Photograph: Milford Lewis.

KILCREENE HOUSE, Kilkenny

A very important late seventeenth-century house. It had a 'H' shaped plan. Flanking screen walls were added to the entrance front in the eighteenth century and a single storey porch was added in the nineteenth century. Very fine interior with interesting early eighteenth-century chimney-pieces. The house was sold in 1947 and has since been demolished. Seat of General Drummond in 1814. Some chimney-pieces survive at nearby Bonnettstown Hall and Kilcreene Lodge.

MULLINABRO, Kilmacow

A two storey Georgian house. In 1814 the seat of Humphrey Jones.   Now a ruin.

NEWPARK HOUSE

A large, late eighteenth-century, three storey house built by the Newport family of Waterford. Good pedimented Doric doorcase. Burnt in 1932.

NEWTOWN HOUSE, Kells

An early nineteenth-century house.   Now a ruin.

WELLINGTON, Kells

A two storey early nineteenth-century house.   Now a ruin.

WOODSGIFT, Urlingford

A large, three storey, mid to late eighteenth-century house. Porch added in the nineteenth century. In 1814 the seat of Sir Richard St. George. Burnt c.1914.   Ruin now demolished.

WOODSTOCK, Inistioge

A large three storey house built in the 1740's for Sir Edward Fownes to the design of Francis Bindon. The front doorcase was altered in the late eighteenth-century or early nineteenth-century and single storey pedimented wings were added. Burnt c.1920. Now a ruin.

Facing page:
Newpark House: Entrance front 1898.
Photograph: J.W. Lapham.
Collection: Maj. R.J.H. Carew on loan to the Irish Architectural Archive.

Top right:
Bellevue: Entrance front.
Old photograph.

Above:
Woodstock: Front doorcase, 1959.
Photograph: Hugh Doran.

Bottom right:
Castlecomer House: Entrance front.
Photograph: Gillman Collection.

Woodsgift:
Property defence expedition encamped near house, September 1881.
Photograph: Lawrence Studio, Dublin.

COUNTY LEITRIM

DERRYCARNE, Dromod
A two storey late Georgian house. The seat of M. Nesbett in 1814.   Derelict.

DRUMHIERNEY, Leitrim
A two storey rendered house. Conservatory with fluted Ionic pilasters.   Derelict.

KINLOUGH HOUSE, Kinlough
An attractive early nineteenth-century house with a single storey Doric portico built by Robert Johnston.
Now a ruin.

LAKEFIELD, Mohill
A late Georgian house with a good Ionic doorcase. The seat of Edward Hanley in 1814.
Derelict.

Kinlough House: Entrance front 1974.
Photograph: William Garner

Oldderrig: Entrance front c.1975.
Photograph: William Garner.

COUNTY LEIX

AHARNEY, Durrow
An interesting, mid nineteenth-century, single storey house with a two storey tower at one end. Built by Edward Marum. Now a ruin.

BALLAGHMORE, Ballaghmore
A late seventeenth-century or early eighteenth-century gable-ended house.   Now a ruin.

BELLEGROVE, Ballybrittas
A large early nineteenth-century house. An Italianate Romanesque winter garden was added later in the nineteenth century to the design of T.M. Deane. The house was burnt in 1922.

BROCKLEY PARK, Stradbally
A large three storey house built in 1768 to the design of Davis Duckart for the 2nd Viscount Jocelyn, later 1st Earl of Roden. Additions were made in the nineteenth century. Superb interior plasterwork and staircase. Dismantled in 1944, some ruins remain.

COOLRAIN HOUSE, Coolrain
An early to mid eighteenth-century gable-ended house. Good Gibbsian doorcase.   Now a ruin.

DUNMORE, Durrow
A three storey, gable-ended, early eighteenth-century house with projecting two storey wings. A ruin for many years. The seat of the Staples family.   Demolished.

GLENMALIRE HOUSE, Ballybrittas
A two storey early nineteenth-century house.   Derelict.

GRANTSTON MANOR, Abbeyleix
A two storey early nineteenth-century house with a single storey Doric porch. The interior was much altered in the late nineteenth century and early twentieth century. In 1814 the seat of William Hayes.   The house was gutted by fire in 1977.

HEYWOOD, Ballinakill
A superb house built in 1773 by M.F. Trench who may also have designed it, James Gandon may also have been involved.

Much altered and enlarged in the nineteenth century. The house was destroyed by fire in 1950 and the ruins have since been demolished.

KILMORNEY, Ballylynan
A plain early nineteenth-century house. In 1814 the seat of Stewart Weldon.   Now a ruin.

KNAPTON, Abbeyleix
A fine late eighteenth-century two storey house with good interior. In 1814 the seat of Mrs. Morton.   Demolished.

KNOCKNATRINA HOUSE, Durrow
A large mid Victorian Gothic house, burnt in 1940. Now a ruin.

LAMBERTON PARK, Stradbally
A two storey house. Seat of the Moore family.   Demolished.

LANSDOWNE PARK, Portarlington
A large, plain, two storey, early nineteenth-century, gable-ended house.   Derelict.

OLDERRIG HOUSE, Clonmore
A three storey, gable-ended, early eighteenth-century house with a pedimented doorcase. In 1814 the seat of Benjamin Galbraith. Derelict.

RYNN, Rosenallis
A house built in 1855 for John Rynne.   Demolished.

THORNBERRY HOUSE, Abbeyleix
A two storey early nineteenth-century house. In 1814 the seat of Francis Evans.   Derelict.

TINNAKILL HOUSE, Abbeyleix
A two storey, pedimented, late eighteenth-century and early nineteenth-century house.   Derelict.

WESTFIELDFARM, Castletown
In 1814 the seat of John Price.   Demolished.

Facing page:
Top:
Knocknatrina.
Photograph: William Garner 1986.

Bottom left:
Brockley Park: Drawing room ceiling.
Photograph c.1944.

Bottom right:
Heywood: Entrance front.
Photograph: Gillman Collection.

Above:
Dunmore: Entrance front.
Old photograph.

Right:
Glenmalire House: Entrance front 1986.
Photograph: William Garner.

Mount Shannon: Entrance front c.1900.
Copy photograph: William Garner.

COUNTY LIMERICK

ASHBURN, Limerick city
An eighteenth-century house to which a three bay, two storey front was added in 1829. Entrance door with an attractive semi-circular Roman Ionic portico.   Demolished.

BALLYNAGUARDE, Ballyneety
A very large house built in 1774 and having early nineteenth-century additions. The seat of the Crokers.   Now a ruin.

BALLYNOE, Ballingarry
Late eighteenth-century house with nineteenth-century roof built for Hugh Cox.   Derelict.

CAHERLINE, Castleconnell
An attractive, early nineteenth-century, single storey villa with a very fine but slightly later cast iron veranda.   Now a ruin.

CAHIR-GUILLAMORE, Kilmallock
A two storey late seventeenth or early eighteenth-century house with projecting end bays. High-pitched roof with dormer windows. Former seat of the O'Grady family.   Now a ruin.

CASTLE OLIVER (also known as CLONODFOY), Kilfinane
Scottish baronial castle designed by G. Fowler Jones of York in 1850 for the Misses Oliver-Gascoigne.   Derelict.

COOPER HILL, Clarina
Two storey, six bay, pedimented house built in 1741. Very fine Roman Doric doorcase with segmental pediment. Seat of the Coopers.   Demolished.

CURRAGH CHASE, Adare
A mid Georgian house with large early nineteenth-century additions designed by Amon Henry Wilds. The house was destroyed by fire in 1941. Both the ruins and the grounds are maintained by the Department of Lands.

DEVON CASTLE
A plain two storey Georgian house.   Demolished.

DROMORE CASTLE, Pallaskenry
One of the most important Victorian houses in the country.

Designed by Edward William Godwin for the 3rd Earl of Limerick and built between 1867 and 1870. Godwin incorporates details which he had seen and studied in Irish buildings of the fifteenth and sixteenth centuries and earlier. The three storey main block has a tall keep at one end and a copy of a round tower at the other. The house was dismantled in the 1950's and remains one of the most spectacular ruins in Ireland. The present owner has plans to re-roof and restore it.

ELM PARK, Clarina
A large, cut stone, early nineteenth-century, castellated house of two and three storeys.   Demolished.

FORT ELIZABETH, Croom
A plain, two storey, five bay, gable-ended house.   Derelict.

GLENDUFF CASTLE, Broadford
An early nineteenth-century castellated house.   Now a ruin.

GLEN VIEW, Ballyneety   Demolished.

GRANGE (THE), Sixmilebridge
A three storey, six bay, late eighteenth-century house rendered in the nineteenth century. Remains of good plasterwork. In 1814 the seat of Standish O'Grady.   Now a ruin.

GREENMOUNT, Patrickswell
A plain early nineteenth-century house. Seat of the Green family. Demolished. A new house designed by Donal O'Neill Flanagan stands on the site.

GROVE, Ballingarry   Demolished, but stables remain.

HERMITAGE, Castleconnell
A very fine house built in 1800 for the Bruce family. Elevation with Coade stone decoration. Good interior including an oval entrance hall. A ruin for many years, now demolished. New house on site.

KILBALLYOWEN, Bruff
A two storey late eighteenth-century, early nineteenth-century house incorporating an old castle. Fine entrance hall with screen of columns at one end. Superb drawing-room which retained its early nineteenth-century curtains and wallpaper. Seat of the O'Gradys. The house was still standing in 1968. This was demolished, and a new house has since been built.

LINFIELD, Pallasgreen
A large, three storey, late eighteenth-century, brick house. In 1814 the seat of M.M. Apjohn.   Now a ruin.

Above left:
Springfield Castle: Dining room after fire, 1923.

Above right:
Cooper Hill: Front doorcase 1974.
Photograph: William Garner.

Right:
Cahir-Guillamore: Entrance front 1965.
Copy photograph: David Davison.

Facing page:
Dromore Castle: Drawing room chimneypiece 1986.
Photograph: William Garner.

MOUNT SHANNON, Castleconnell
A magnificent late eighteenth-century house remodelled *c.*1813 to the design of Lewis Wyatt for John FitzGibbon, 1st Earl of Clare. Entrance front with two storey Ionic portico. Severe Greek Revival interior.   Now a ruin.

RAWLEYSTOWN COURT, Herbertstown   Now a ruin.

RIDDLESTOWN PARK, Rathkeale
A three storey house built *c.*1730. A plain version of nearby Mount Ievers Court and probably designed by a member of the Rothery family. In 1814 the seat of G. Blennerhasset. Now semi-derelict.

ROCKBARTON, Bruff
A large, three storey, late Georgian house with single storey Roman Ionic porch.   Now a ruin.

RYVES CASTLE, Knocklong
Demolished.

SPRINGFIELD CASTLE, Dromcolliher
A large, three storey, early eighteenth-century house with a high-pitched roof, former seat of the FitzMaurice family. Dining-room

redecorated in the late eighteenth century. The house was destroyed by fire in 1923 and has been demolished except for the tower house which it incorporated at the rere and the early nineteenth-century service wing which was rebuilt and extended to form the present house.

TERVOE, Clarina
Large, three storey, seven bay house built in 1776 for Col. W.T. Monsell M.P., to which a single storey Ionic portico and single storey wings were added in the early nineteenth century. The interior contained good plasterwork and very fine mahogany doors to the principal room. There was an oval music-room in one of the wings which had a coved ceiling. Dismantled *c.*1953. Some of the fittings are now at Glin Castle. Portico now at Mungret College, Co. Limerick.   Ruin demolished.

Below:
Curragh Chase: Garden front 1938.

Facing, top:
Hermitage: Entrance front c.1900.
Photograph: Collection Charles Guinness.

Facing, bottom:
Rockbarton: Entrance front c.1900.

Above:

Tervoe: Entrance front c.1945.
Photograph: Standish Stewart. Copy photograph: David Davison.

Right:

Castle Oliver.
Old photograph.

COUNTY LONGFORD

DOORY HALL, Ballymahon
A two storey, five bay, late Georgian house with a single storey
Doric portico. Designed by John Hargrave for Mrs Jessop.
Now a ruin.

FARRAGH, Longford
A large, cut stone, Georgian house enlarged between 1811 and
1833 by John Hargrave of Cork for Willoughby Bond.
Demolished 1960's.

FOX HALL, Lenamore
Built for the Fox family.   Now a ruin.

LISARD, Edgeworthstown
Unusual late eighteenth-century house with an interesting

entrance elevation of two storeys with a blind mezzanine between
them. Side elevation of three floors within the same overall
height. The principal front had fine quality cut stone detailing.
The house incorporates the remains of an earlier late seventeenth-
century or early eighteenth-century building.
Demolished *c.*1950.

MOSSTOWN, Ballymahon
Very important, large, seventeenth-century, gable-ended house
with early Georgian alterations. The high-pitched roof had
attractive early eighteenth-century pedimented dormer-windows
and massive chimney-stacks. The interior contained early
eighteenth-century panelled rooms and a good staircase.
Demolished in the early 1960's.

MOUNT JESSOP, Longford
A very plain, three storey, gable-ended, eighteenth-century house
built for the Jessop family.   Derelict.

WHITE HILL, Edgeworthstown
A two storey, castellated, Victorian house built for the Wilson-
Slator family.   Demolished *c.*1961.

Mosstown: Entrance front.
Old photograph.

Above:
Ravensdale Park: Library.
Right: *Rere view.*
Photographs: Gillman Collection. Copy photographs: David Davison.

COUNTY LOUTH

COLLON RECTORY, Collon
A three storey early to mid Georgian house. Roof altered in the nineteenth century. Good pedimented doorcase. The house was derelict for many years and has recently been demolished. The doorcase was saved.

CORBOLLIS, Tallanstown
A three storey late eighteenth-century house with single storey Ionic portico. In 1814 the seat of T. Lee Norman. Demolished.

GREENMOUNT LODGE, Kilsaron
A late eighteenth-century house. The seat of Turner Macan in 1814.   Now a ruin.

PIEDMONT, Bush
Five bay, two storey, early eighteenth-century, gable-ended house. Two projecting wings at rere making a 'U' plan. Now a ruin.

RAVENSDALE PARK, Dundalk
A two storey, Italianate, early Victorian house designed by Thomas Duff for Thomas Fortescue, 1st Lord Clermont. Good interior. Burnt 1920.   Demolished.

STEPHENSTOWN, Dundalk
A large late eighteenth-century house to which wings were added in the early nineteenth century. Built for the Fortescue family. One wing was later demolished. Good interior.
The house is now derelict.

COUNTY MAYO

BINGHAM CASTLE, Belmullet
A large symmetrical early nineteenth-century castle. Seat of the Bingham family.   Now a ruin.

BLOOMFIELD, Claremorris
An early Georgian house enlarged *c.*1769. The house was further altered in the late eighteenth century and early nineteenth century. Good interior. In 1814 the seat of Robert Rutledge. Demolished.

CARROWMORE, Killala
Two storey late eighteenth-century house.   Now a ruin.

CASTLEBAR HOUSE, Castlebar
A small early nineteenth-century house built to replace that destroyed in the 1798 rebellion. John B. Papworth of London prepared designs for this house in 1825 and it is not known if he was the architect of the modest house that was built. Seat of the Earls of Lucan.   Destroyed by fire.

CASTLE GORE (Old Castle, formerly DEEL CASTLE), Ballina
A sixteenth-century tower house with a wing added in the mid eighteenth century. This wing has a simple rusticated doorcase. Seat of the Gore family, afterwards Earls of Arran.
Now a ruin.

CASTLE GORE, Ballina
A large plain house built *c.*1790 for James Cuff M.P., 1st Lord Tyrawley. The house was severely damaged in the 1798 rebellion. Very fine granite Doric pedimented doorcase. Burnt in 1922.   Now a ruin.

CASTLE LACKIN, Ballycastle
A plain, two storey, late eighteenth-century and early nineteenth-century house. In 1814 the seat of Lord Tyrawley.
Now a ruin.

CASTLEREA, Killala
A plain, two storey, late eighteenth-century and early nineteenth-century house demolished in 1937. Seat of the Knox family. Part of a crenellated stable wall remains.

CLOGHER HOUSE, Ballyglass
A large, three storey, late eighteenth-century house with a good tripartite granite Tuscan pedimented doorcase. Good plasterwork in entrance hall and drawing-room. Recently destroyed by fire. Now a ruin.

GREENWOOD PARK, Ballina
A two storey late Georgian house built by Major John Knox. Dismantled 1961.   Now a ruin.

HOLLYMOUNT HOUSE, Hollymount
An eighteenth-century two storey house. Refaced *c.*1834 to the design of George Papworth for Thomas Spencer Lindsey. Now a ruin.

KILLALA CASTLE, Killala
Former palace of the Church of Ireland Bishop of Killala. A very plain, three storey, mid to late eighteenth-century block with later additions.   Demolished in the 1950's.

LACKEN (GLEBE HOUSE), Killala
A two storey early eighteenth-century house.   Now a ruin.

MOORE HALL, Ballyglass
A large three storey house built in 1795 for George Moore. The house is similar to Tyrone House Co. Galway. Burnt in 1923. Now a ruin which has been stabilised.

NEALE (THE), Ballinrobe
A two storey early to mid eighteenth-century house. The roof was altered in the mid nineteenth century. A large wing was added *c.*1907 by 5th Lord Kilmaine. The house was demolished *c.*1939.   Some follies remain.

NETLEY PARK, Ballina
An attractive, two storey, early nineteenth-century house with a rusticated tripartite doorcase. Built for Captain H.W. Knox. Dismantled in 1962.   Now a ruin.

NEWBROOK, Claremorris
A large, two storey, late eighteenth-century house for the Bingham family. Very fine rusticated and pedimented Doric doorcase.   The house was destroyed by fire in 1837.

RAHINS, Castlebar
Plain, two storey, early nineteenth-century, pedimented house. Seat of the Browne family.   Now a ruin.

RAPPA CASTLE, Ballina
A late seventeenth-century gable-ended house with diagonal

chimney-stacks. In 1814 the seat of Annesley Knox. Dismantled 1937.   Now a ruin.

SUMMER HILL, Killala

A very interesting and attractive, mid eighteenth-century, pedimented and gable-ended house. A two storey wing was added at a later date. The roof is of interest in that it is covered with sandstone slabs rather than slates. In 1814 the seat of Thomas Palmer.   Derelict.

TOWERHILL, Ballyglass

A late eighteenth-century, two storey, pedimented house. Good interior plasterwork. Seat of the Blakes.   Now a ruin.

Towerhill: Entrance front c.1975.
Photograph: William Garner.

COUNTY MEATH

ARCH HALL, Wilkinstown
A very interesting early eighteenth-century house attributed to Sir Edward Lovett Pearce. The house is in fact a smaller version of Wardstown Co. Donegal. The top floor was altered during the first half of the nineteenth century. In 1814 the seat of J.N. Payne Garnett.   Now a ruin.

ATHCARNE CASTLE, Duleek
A tower house with a three storey early nineteenth-century wing. In 1814 the seat of Henry Garnett.   Now a ruin.

BLACK CASTLE, Navan
Very fine, two storey, early nineteenth-century house. Entrance front with single storey Doric portico.
Recently destroyed by fire.

CLONABREANY, Crossakeel
An early nineteenth-century house of which only two wings in ruins remain. Superb pedimented stable block nearby. In 1814 the seat of Robert Wade.

DANGAN CASTLE, Trim
A two storey early to mid eighteenth-century house incorporating an earlier house. The seat of the Wesley (later changed to Wellesley) family.   In ruins since the early nineteenth century.

DOOLISTOWN, Trim
A two storey house with a good doorcase.   Now a ruin.

DOLLARDSTOWN, Slane
A superb house remodelled *c.*1730 for Arthur Meredyth probably to the design of Richard Castle but incorporating a late seventeenth-century house. Very fine interior plasterwork and main staircase. The house was still roofed in the 1950's and having stood as a ruin for many years was demolished in 1986. The cut stone doorcase and other details were saved and are now in a private collection in Co. Cork.

GIBBSTOWN, Navan
A large, three storey, Victorian, Italianate house. Single storey Doric entrance portico. The entrance hall had plasterwork panels of the four seasons by Samuel Ferris Lynn (1834-1876), brother

of the architect W.H. Lynn. Gutted by fire in the early twentieth century and rebuilt. The stonework is now in store at New Mellifont House, Co. Louth.   Demolished *c.*1960.

GLENFARM
A two storey, gable-ended, early nineteenth-century house. Derelict.

HARBOURSTOWN, Fourknocks
A very attractive, two storey, early nineteenth-century house with a single storey Ionic portico. Built for R.C. O'Farrell. The original architect's model for the house survives in store at Castletown Co. Kildare.   The house has been demolished.

KILBREW, Ratoath In ruins.

KILBRIDE
A gable-ended seventeenth-century house altered in the eighteenth century, now forming a wing to a mid-Victorian, two storey, pedimented house with a single storey Ionic portico. Now a ruin.

KILLEEN CASTLE, Dunsany
A tower house altered and enlarged *c.*1804 for 8th Earl of Fingall to the design of Francis Johnston. The castle was again enlarged in 1841, the architect being James Sheil. Very fine interior by Johnston and Sheil. The castle was sold in the early 1950's and remained unoccupied (but maintained) until its destruction by fire in 1981.   Now a ruin.
Facing page: Staircase c.1975. Photograph by William Garner.

KINGSFORT, Moynalty
A two storey house of *c.*1740 with early nineteenth-century additions at the rere. The ground floor rooms of the original house have brick vaulted ceilings as at Ballyhaise Co. Cavan. The seat of Richard Chalener in 1814.   Now a ruin.

LISMULLEN (eighteenth-century house), Skreen
A three storey early eighteenth-century house much altered. The top storey may be a later addition. Burnt in 1922. Demolished.

LOUGHCREW, Oldcastle
A superb Greek Revival house built in 1823 for J.L. Naper to the design of C.R. Cockerell. A large service wing was added 1823-1825. After a fire in 1888 the house was rebuilt without the attic storey. The house was destroyed by another fire in *c.*1960 and was not rebuilt.
Some ruins remain. A superb gate lodge and stable block remain and the conservatory has recently been restored as a house.

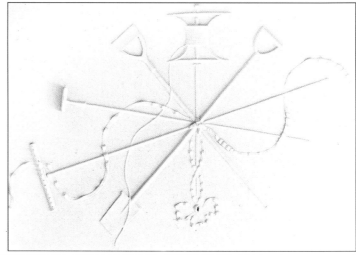

Above:

Randlestown: Entrance front.
Old photograph, Gillman Collection. Copy photograph: David Davison.

Right: *Library ceiling detail c.1975.*
Photograph: William Garner.

Facing, left:
Platten Hall: Dining room c.1915.
Photograph: Milford Lewis.

Facing, right:
Tirachorka: Entrance front 1978.
Photograph: William Garner.

NEWGROVE, Kells

A two storey, late eighteenth-century, gable-ended house with cut stone pedimented centre piece, now removed. The seat of Philip Reilly in 1814.   The house is now a ruin.

PLATTEN HALL, Donore

Very important, three storey, early eighteenth-century house attributed to Sir William Robinson. The top floor was removed in the early nineteenth century. Very fine interior which included a superb staircase and a panelled dining-room. Built for Alderman John Graham. The dining-room was re-erected in a house in Dublin.   The house was demolished c.1950.

RANDLESTOWN, Navan

A two storey early eighteenth-century house for Lt.-Col. Mathias Everard to which a third storey was added c.1780 when the original entrance front became the garden front. Good late eighteenth-century plasterwork on main staircase.
Recently demolished.

ROCK LODGE

A two storey early nineteenth-century house with later additions. Demolished.

RUSK, Dunboyne

A three storey, gable-ended, early eighteenth-century house with a two storey early nineteenth-century projection containing the entrance door.   Now a ruin.

SUMMERHILL, Summerhill

A superb house probably designed by Sir Edward Lovett Pearce in collaboration with Richard Castle who carried it out after Pearce's death. The house was built in 1731 for Hercules Rowley M.P. The arched chimney-stacks of the main block show the influence of Sir John Vanburgh.

The house was damaged by two fires in the nineteenth-century but some plasterwork by the Francini brothers survived. The house was burnt in 1922. Having stood as a magnificent ruin for many years, the stonework was sold and the ruin demolished c.1962. Only the flanking pedimented arches and screen walls survive.

SYLVAN PARK, Kells

A three storey early nineteenth-century house now demolished. In 1814 the seat of Walter Keating. Very attractive stables survive.

TIRACHORKA, Moynalty

A fine, two storey, pedimented, gable-ended, late eighteenth-century house.   Now a ruin.

TRIMLESTOWN CASTLE, Kildalkey

An eighteenth-century house incorporating a tower house. The building was further altered in the early nineteenth century. Now a ruin.

WILLIAMSTON, Kells

A very fine, three storey, cut stone house originally of five bays but extended to nine in the early nineteenth century in the same style. The original house was built c.1760-70. In 1814 the seat of John Otway.
For many years unoccupied.

Above:
Williamston: Entrance front c.1975.
Photograph: William Garner.

Right:
Loughcrew: Entrance front c.1860.
Hamilton Collection.

Facing, top:
Athcarne Castle: Entrance front c.1975.
Photograph: William Garner.

Facing, bottom:
Summerhill: Entrance front.
Photograph: Maurice Craig.

Above:
Dartrey: Garden front.
Old photograph.

Facing page:
Rossmore Park.
Old postcard. Gillman Collection.

COUNTY MONAGHAN

CAMLA VALE, Monaghan
Attractive, large, late Georgian, single storey house built for Lt.-Col. Henry Westenra. Good interior. Sold in 1962 and since demolished.

CASTLE SHANE, Monaghan
A large, three storey, Jacobean style house built in 1836 for the Lucas family.   Burnt in 1920.

COOLDERRY HOUSE, Carrickmacross
A two storey, bow fronted, late Georgian house. Built by the Brownlows.   Demolished but some traces remain.

CORNACASSA, Monaghan
Very fine, cut stone, two storey, early nineteenth-century house with a single storey Doric portico built for Dacre Hamilton. Demolished but the stables remain.

DARTREY, Rockcorry
A large, two storey, Elizabethan Revival house built in 1846 to the design of William Burn for Richard Dawson, later first Lord Dartry. Demolished c. 1950.
A superb but now roofless mausoleum designed by James Wyatt survives in the park.

GOLA, Scotstown
A curious, early to mid eighteenth-century, two storey, gable-ended house with a central tower with pyramidal roof. The seat of William Wright in 1814.
Burnt in 1920 and since demolished.

ROSSMORE PARK, Monaghan
A large Tudor Revival house built in 1827 to the design of William Vitruvius Morrison for 2nd Lord Rossmore.
The house was altered and enlarged in 1858 to the design of William H. Lynn.
A ruin for many years now demolished.

COUNTY OFFALY

BALLYBURLY, Edenderry
An important, two storey, late seventeenth-century or early eighteenth-century house built for John Wakely or his son Thomas.   Burnt in 1888.

BALLYLIN, Ferbane
A fine, late eighteenth-century, two storey house much altered in the late nineteenth-century and early twentieth-century when a single storey porch was added. Built for the King family. Demolished.

BALLYRIHY, Dunkerrin
Now a ruin.

CLONEARL, Philipstown
A very fine, cut stone, two storey house built for W.H. Magan to the design of William Farrell *c.*1817. Garden front with two storey Ionic portico in antis.
Demolished.

CUBA COURT, Banagher
An important early eighteenth-century house of the school of Sir Edward Lovett Pearce for the Fraser family. Dismantled 1946. Now a ruin.

FFRANCKFORT CASTLE, Dunkerrin
An early nineteenth-century, three storey, castellated house incorporating an earlier castle. Built for the Rolleston family. Demolished.

GARRYHINCH, Portarlington
A three storey early eighteenth-century house with a late eighteenth-century pedimented doorcase built for the Warburton family. Burnt in 1914.   Demolished.

GEASHILL, Geashill
A late Georgian house altered in the mid nineteenth century. Burnt in 1922.

GORTNAMONA (formerly MOUNT PLEASANT), Tullamore
A three storey late eighteenth-century house. Built for the O'Connor family. Burnt in 1922.   Now a ruin.

HOLLOW HOUSE, Tullamore
A very attractive and rare example of a single storey thatched gentleman's house with well finished interiors. The house stands in the bawn of an earlier castle.   Derelict.

LEAP CASTLE, Coolderry
A large tower house altered and enlarged c.1750 by Jonathan Darby, who added two storey battlement wings and the Gothic front doorcase in the style of Batty Langley.
Destroyed by fire in 1922 and now in ruins. The present owner hopes to restore it.

LEIPSIC HOUSE, Shinrone
Attractive, two storey, early nineteenth-century house with modern gabled porch.   Derelict.

MOUNT LUCAS, Cruachan
A three storey, early eighteenth-century, gable-ended house with later wings built for the Lucas family.   Demolished.

RATHROBIN, Tullamore
Nineteenth-century Tudor Revival house designed by Sir Thomas Drew for the Biddulph family. Burnt *c.*1920. Now a ruin.

THOMASTOWN, Birr
Built for the Leggat family in the mid eighteenth century. Demolished.

Facing page:
Cuba Court: Entrance front 1978.
Photograph: William Garner.

Above:
Ffranckfort Castle: Entrance front.
Photograph: Standish Stewart. Copy photograph: David Davison.

Left:
Ballyburly: Entrance front.
Old photograph.

Above:

Leipsic House: Entrance front c.1984.
Photograph: John Colclough.

Above:

Thomastown House:
Entrance front in process of demolition, 1958.

Facing page:
Elphin, Bishop's Palace: Entrance front.
Old photograph.

COUNTY ROSCOMMON

BALLANAGARE, Ballanagare
Very interesting, single storey, pedimented, early eighteenth-century house. Fine doorcase. Two projecting wings at rere built by the O'Conors.   Now a ruin.

CASTLEREA HOUSE, Castlerea
Very large, eighteenth-century, three storey house. Two storey wing added in nineteenth century when the entrance doorway was moved to one end of the house. The roof of the original house was also altered at this time. The seat of the Sandford family. Demolished.

CLAREMOUNT, Claremorris
Plain two storey early nineteenth-century house.   Derelict.

CLONALIS (eighteenth-century house), Castlerea
A two storey, gable-ended, early eighteenth-century house, seat of the O'Conor Don. Single storey wings were added at a later date and the roof was altered in the early nineteenth century when a porch was also added. A new house was built *c.* 1880 but the old house was retained.
Derelict after storm damage in 1961.

CLOONYQUIN, Elphin
A plain, two storey, Georgian house built for the French family. It was extended at various times.   Demolished.

ELPHIN BISHOP'S PALACE, Elphin
A large, early to mid eighteenth-century house, similar in style to the work of Richard Castle. Two storey pavilions joined to main block by curved sweeps as at nearby French Park. Main block demolished, wings remain.   Derelict.

FRENCH PARK, French Park
Three storey house built for John French *c.* 1730 probably to the design of Richard Castle. Two storey pavilions joined to main block by plain curved sweeps. Good interior much altered in the late eighteenth century and early nineteenth century when a single storey portico was added to the entrance front. Interior dismantled in the 1950's. Ruin demolished *c.* 1970. Dining-room chimney-piece now in a private collection in Co. Cork. Entrance gates now at Leixlip House Co. Kildare.

Above:
Mount Plunkett: Entrance front c.1920.
Photograph: William English. Copy photograph: David Davison.

Right:
Kilronan Castle: Garden front c.1858.
Photograph by Edward King Tenison. Collection: Nat. Library of Ireland.

Facing page:
French Park: Entrance front 1954.
Photograph: National Parks & Monuments Branch, Commrs. of Public Works.

KILRONAN CASTLE, Ballyfarnan

A three storey early nineteenth-century castle built for the Tennison family. Large additions made *c.*1860, including a porte-cochère and a tower.   Now a ruin.

MANTUA, Castlerea

A three storey house built *c.*1747 to the design of Richard Castle for Oliver Grace. Elevation of main block similar to that of the same architect's Waterford Bishop's Palace. The flanking wings and link arcades were demolished in the nineteenth century when the roof of the main block was also altered. A single storey porch was added at a later date.   Derelict.

MOTE PARK, Ballymurray

A three storey house designed by Richard Morrison for the Croftons, incorporating a late eighteenth-century house. The house was destroyed by fire in 1865 and rebuilt with minor alterations.   Demolished *c.*1958.

MOUNT PLUNKETT, Athlone

A most unusual house built in 1806 for George Plunkett. Five bay entrance front with three bay, two storey centre. The end bays were of three storeys in height forming towers. Dismantled 1946.   Now a ruin.

MOUNT TALBOT, Athleague

A mid eighteenth-century Palladian house built for the Talbots consisting of a central block connected to pavilions by open arcade sweeps. The pavilions have elevations similar to those at Altaville Co. Limerick. In *c.*1820, the central block was remodelled in the Tudor Revival style. The house was burnt in 1922, but the arcade and wings remain.

ROCKINGHAM, Boyle

A two storey classical house built in 1810 to the design of John Nash for General Robert King, 1st Viscount Lorton; in 1822 an extra storey was added. The house was damaged by fire *c.*1863 and rebuilt. Very fine interior including a top-lit inner hall and a stone imperial staircase.

The house was destroyed by fire in 1957 and has since been demolished.

ROCKVILLE, Elphin

An early to mid nineteenth-century house built by Owen Lloyd. Demolished.

RUNNAMOAT, Ballymore

A three storey late eighteenth-century house. The seat of the Chichesters.   Burnt in 1933.

THOMASTOWN HOUSE, Athlone

A three storey early eighteenth-century house. Roof altered in the early nineteenth century when a Doric porch was also added. Demolished 1958.

Facing page:
Mantua: Main staircase 1972.
Photograph: J & S Harsch.

Above:
Rockingham: Entrance front c.1890.
Photograph: Robert French. Lawrence Collection, Nat. Library of Ireland.

Right:
Mote Park: Entrance front c.1860 before fire.
Photograph: Augusta Crofton.

COUNTY SLIGO

ABBEYVILLE, Ballymote
A two storey house built in 1716 for William Phibbs, altered 1816.   Fell into ruin in the late nineteenth century.

CASTLE NEYNOE, Ballintogher
A late eighteenth-century Gothic castle with a crenellated tower. Now a romantic ruin.

Facing page:
Markree Castle: Entrance hall 1986.
Photograph: William Garner.

CASTLETOWN, Easky
Demolished.

LISHEEN, Ballysadare
A large, two storey, classical house designed by John Benson in 1842 for William Phibbs. Dismantled 1940.
Now a ruin.

MARKREE CASTLE, Collooney
An eighteenth-century house transformed into a castle to the design of Francis Johnston in 1802. Further enlargement took place in 1866 to the design of James Maitland Wardrop for Joshua Cooper. Very little of Johnston's interior survives. Derelict.

Below:
Markree Castle: Entrance front.
Photograph: c.1860, Gillman Collection.

COUNTY TIPPERARY

AHERLOW CASTLE, Bansha
A small, early nineteenth-century, castellated house built for the Moore family of Mooresfort.   Demolished.

BALLYNACOURTY, Ballysteen
Curious, two storey, early nineteenth-century, cut stone house with a three storey octagonal tower at one end.   Demolished.

BARNANE, Templemore
A large, two storey, early to mid nineteenth-century, Tudor Revival house.   Now a ruin.

CAHIR PARK, Cahir
Very poor baronial house built in 1861 to the design of Lanyon, Lynn & Lanyon for Lady Margaret Charteris.   Burnt 1961.

CASTLE FFOGARTY, Thurles
A large, two storey, early nineteenth-century castle, built for the Ffogartys and destroyed by fire in 1922.   In ruins.

CASTLE OTWAY, Templedeery
A fine, mid Georgian, two storey, pedimented house. Good Doric pedimented doorcase. A tower house much altered is incorporated at the rere of the house; built for the Otways; burnt in 1922.   Now a ruin.

CASTLE SHEPPARD, Borrisokane
Small, plain, two storey, mid to late eighteenth-century house. Very fine Chinese Chippendale staircase.   Derelict.

DERRY CASTLE (eighteenth-century house), Ballina
Very fine, three storey, late eighteenth-century, bow fronted house. Good Ionic pedimented doorcase.   Demolished.

Facing page:
Gortkelly Castle:
Entrance front c.1975.
Photograph: William Garner.

Below:
Aherlow Castle.
Photograph: William Garner c.1975.

DERRYLAHAN PARK, Riverstown

A high Victorian house designed by Sir Thomas Newenham Deane in 1862 for William H. Head.   Burnt in 1921.

GALTEE CASTLE, Clogheen

A nineteenth-century castle built for Abel Buckley M.P. Dismantled *c.*1940.

GORTKELLY CASTLE, Annfield

Symmetrical, early nineteenth-century, castellated house. Now a ruin.

GRALLAGH CASTLE (new), Cashel

Demolished, but stables remain.

GREENHILLS, Roscrea

A three storey late eighteenth-century house with a pedimented Doric doorcase.   Now a ruin.

JOHNSTOWN (formerly PETERFIELD), Puckaun

Three storey late eighteenth-century house probably designed by William Leeson for Peter Holmes M.P. Good plasterwork. Now a ruin.

KILBOY (eighteenth-century house), Nenagh

The most important house designed by William Leeson *c.*1780 for Henry Prittie M.P., 1st Lord Dunalley. Superb entrance front with engaged Doric portico. Very fine interior with good plasterwork and imperial main staircase. The house was burnt in 1922 and well restored but without the attic storey. In the mid 1950's it was demolished and a single storey house was built on top of the basement storey; reached by the original steps.

LISHEEN CASTLE, Templemore

An early to mid nineteenth-century, rather severe, Gothic castle built for the Lloyd family. Burnt in 1900 and now a well preserved ruin.

Below:
Rochestown: Entrance front c.1860.

Facing, top:
Thomastown Castle: Entrance front 1917.
Collection: Miss Moira Lysaght.

Facing, bottom*: Entrance front c.1969.*
Photograph: Christopher Tynne.

LISSEN HALL, Nenagh

A fine, two storey, mid Georgian, pedimented house similar to Castle Otway in the same county. Very fine arched doorcase; built by the Otway family.   Now a ruin.

LITTLEFIELD, Urlingford

An attractive and fine, early eighteenth-century, gable-ended house; very fine segmental pedimented doorcase.   Derelict.

MOUNTFRISCO, Roscrea

A large, three storey, early eighteenth-century house, the first floor of which seems originally to have been the ground floor. Now a ruin.

NEWCASTLE HOUSE, Newcastle

A plain, two storey, mid eighteenth-century house with early nineteenth-century wings.   Now a ruin.

PORTLAND PARK, Lorrha

Two storey late Georgian house. The seat for the Stoney family. Burnt in 1920.   Now a ruin.

RAPLA, Nenagh

Three storey, mid to late eighteenth-century, pedimented house having a good rusticated doorcase.   Now a ruin.

RICHMOND PARK, Nenagh

Two storey early nineteenth-century house incorporating an earlier house. Partly demolished in 1956.   Now a ruin.

ROCHESTOWN, Cahir

A very fine, two storey, late eighteenth-century or early nineteenth-century house probably designed by Richard Morrison. The house was completely altered in 1867 for the Wise family by Sir Thomas Newenham Deane, architect who added a third storey and a single storey porch.   In ruins.

ROESBOROUGH, Tipperary

A large, two storey, early nineteenth-century house built by James Roe.   Now a ruin.

SHANBALLY CASTLE, Clogheen

John Nash's most important and largest Irish castle. Built *c.*1806 for Cornelius O'Callaghan, 1st Viscount Lismore. The very fine interior included a vaulted entrance hall lit by a series of glass skylights, a splendid oak imperial main staircase and an oval drawing-room.

The castle in good repair was sold in 1954 and despite protests in the press was demolished in 1957. Its destruction was one of Ireland's great architectural losses this century.

TEMPLEMORE ABBEY, Templemore

An early nineteenth-century Tudor Revival house designed by William Vitruvius Morrison for the Carden family and further enlarged later in the century.

Burnt in 1922.

TEMPLEMORE HOUSE, Templemore

Large late eighteenth-century house with engaged, two storey, Doric, pedimented portico. Demolished early nineteenth century and replaced by Templemore Abbey. The seat of the Carden family.

THOMASTOWN CASTLE, Golden

A large Tudor Revival house designed by Richard Morrison in 1812 for Thomas Mathew, 2nd Earl of Llandaff incorporating a late seventeenth-century house which may have been designed by Sir William Robinson.

Very fine interiors some of which were classical.

Now a ruin.

TRAVERSTON, Nenagh

A large, three storey, late eighteenth-century house with a single storey Doric portico. The seat of Thomas Going in the early nineteenth century.

Demolished.

WOODROOFF, Clonmel

A three storey mid eighteenth-century house with superb flanking courts added in the late eighteenth century. The seat of the Perry family.   Now mostly demolished.

Facing page:
Lisheen Castle: Entrance front 1974.
Photograph: William Garner.

Left to right:

Castle Otway: View of entrance and garden fronts.
Old photograph.

Castle Otway: Entrance front 1979.
Photograph: William Garner.

Lissen Hall: Entrance front 1979.
Photograph: William Garner.

Johnstown (formerly Peterfield).
Photograph: Lord Rossmore c.1969.

Derry Castle: Entrance front.
Old photograph.

Above:
Templemore Abbey: Entrance and garden fronts c.1880.
Photograph: Collection Sir John Carden.

Right:
Templemore Abbey: Dining room c.1880.
Photograph: Collection Sir John Carden.

COUNTY WATERFORD

AFFANE, Cappoquin

A plain, late eighteenth- to early nineteenth-century, two storey house. Entrance hall with screen of fluted columns.   Derelict.

ARDO, Ardmore

A late eighteenth-century house to which castellated towers were added in the early nineteenth century. Good classical plasterwork in the stair hall. Built by Jeremiah Coghlan.   Now a ruin.

BALLYCANVAN, Waterford

A two storey late eighteenth-century house added to an old tower house. The seat of the Bolton family. Doorcase now at Georgestown House Co. Waterford.   Now a ruin.

BALLYSAGGARTMORE, Lismore

A late Georgian house with a courtyard built by the Keily family. Demolished. Roofless stables and superb Gothic gates remain.

COOLNAMUCK, Carrickbeg

A three storey eighteenth-century house. The seat of the Wall family.   Demolished.

DROMANA (1780's house), Cappoquin

A two storey house begun c.1780's for George Mason-Villiers, 2nd Earl Grandison but incorporating an earlier house at the rere. The interior was completed in its final form c.1822 by Martin Day architect. Fine interior included a stone imperial staircase and a bow ended drawing-room overlooking the river. The main part of the house was demolished in 1966 and the earlier house was then remodelled to form the present house. The Hindu-Gothic gateway designed by Martin Day in 1849 was restored by the Irish Georgian Society in 1967-68.

DRUMROE HOUSE, Cappoquin

An early nineteenth-century Tudor Revival house.
Now a ruin.

GARRYDUFF, Youghal

A late eighteenth-century house with a pedimented Doric doorcase. The seat of the Garde family.   Now a ruin.

GLENVILLE, Waterford

An Italianate mid nineteenth-century house sold 1957. Demolished following fire damage. Built by the Hassard family.

Dromana: Entrance front c.1900. Photograph: Gillman Collection.

COUNTY WESTMEATH

BALLYNEGALL, Mullingar

Very fine, two storey, classical house with a single storey Ionic entrance portico. Built in 1808 to the design of Francis Johnston for James Gibbons. Fine interior including an entrance hall with a screen of Ionic columns, and a Portland stone staircase with a brass balustrade supporting a mahogany handrail inlaid with brass. The plasterwork in the house was by George Stapleton. Some of the chimney-pieces on the first floor and one in the basement seem to have come from an earlier house. Single storey wings one of which incorporated a conservatory were added in the 1840's. The front elevation of the house was copied *c.*1850 by George Papworth at nearby Middleton Park. The house was stripped in 1981 and the portico was re-erected at Straffan House, Co. Kildare. Some chimney-pieces are now in London. The house is now a ruin.

BARONSTOWN, Ballinacargy

A large, three storey, pedimented house built in 1755 for Richard Malone, 1st Lord Sunderlin, with flanking pavilions joined to the main block by quadrants. The house was rebuilt in 1889, following a fire. Following another fire in 1903 the main block was completely rebuilt to the design of James Franklin Fuller in the Tudor manor house style.   Demolished.

BELVILLE HOUSE, Athlone

Two storey, mid to late eighteenth-century, gable-ended house. In 1814 the seat of William Jones.   Derelict.

CLONLOST, Killucan

Two storey late eighteenth-century house with a three storey pedimented breakfront. The lugged doorcase however seems to be earlier. In 1814 the seat of Lt.-Col. Nugent.   Now a ruin.

CREGGAN, Athlone

Demolished except for two early nineteenth-century Gothic towers.

DERRYMORE, Rathwire

Simple, two storey, pedimented, mid eighteenth-century, gable-ended house. The single storey Doric portico was added in the nineteenth century. In 1814 the seat of Captain Daly. Now a ruin.

DRUMCREE HOUSE, Collinstown

Very attractive, two storey, pedimented, mid eighteenth-century house possibly designed by Michael Wills for the Smyth family. Doorcase with segmental pediment. Interior mostly remodelled in the early nineteenth century when a new main staircase was created. Some original chimney-pieces survive on the first floor. Derelict.

DUNBODEN PARK, Mullingar

Large, two storey, late Georgian house with single storey Doric portico.   Now a ruin. Stables converted to a house.

GAULSTON, Rochfortbridge

A three storey mid to late eighteenth-century house with flanking two storey wings; later Doric porch. Former seat of the Rochforts, burnt in 1920, traces of the garden layout remain. Demolished.

GAULSTOWN, Castle Pollard

A very interesting and attractive, early to mid eighteenth-century, single storey, gable-ended house. Pedimented breakfront with Venetian doorcase, interesting plan. In the eighteenth century the seat of the Hill family.   Derelict.

GAYBROOK, Mullingar

Fine three storey house built in 1790 for the Smyths. Semi-circular Doric portico added in the early nineteenth century. Good interior. Derelict for many years.   Demolished.

GORTMORE, Ballymore

Early nineteenth-century Tudor Revival house.   Now a ruin.

GRANGEMORE, Ratharney

Large, three storey, late Georgian house. In 1814 the seat of John Fetherston.   Now a ruin.

KILDEVIN, Street

Very interesting two storey house built in 1833 with three storey bow in the centre of both front and rere facades. Signed Robert Sproule 1833 above the doorcase, presumably a member of the family of architects and builders of the same name. Interesting plan with oval entrance hall.   Derelict.

KILLUA CASTLE, Clonmellon

Originally a large, three storey, late eighteenth-century, bow fronted house remodelled *c.*1830 possibly to the design of James Shiel when battlements and towers were added. Good interior which included a classical octagonal entrance hall with good plasterwork. Former seat of the Chapmans. A sale of fittings was held in 1944 and the house is now a ruin.

Facing page:
Ballynegall: Drawing room 1961.

Above: *Entrance hall 1961.*
Photographs: Hugh Doran.

LADESTOWN, Mullingar
A two storey house dated 1823 incorporating an earlier eighteenth-century house and a tower house. Very fine well detailed Doric portico. Good interior including a very fine imperial staircase with a screen of fluted Doric columns on the first floor landing. Former seat of the Lyons family.
Derelict for many years.   Demolished.

LILLIPUT, Castletown
A small, two storey, late eighteenth-century house. Good interior plasterwork. In 1814 the seat of Andrew Savage.   Now a ruin.

LONGFIELD, Ballymore
Two storey, early nineteenth-century, Tudor Revival house with single storey porch. The seat of James Longstaff in 1814.
Now a ruin.

LOWTOWN, Kinnegad   Demolished.

MOYDRUM, Athlone
Two storey early nineteenth-century castle built for Lord Castlemaine in 1812 to the design of Richard Morrison; incorporating an earlier house. The interiors were a mixture of Gothic and classical as at Thomastown, Co. Tipperary and Borris, Co. Carlow. The castle was burnt in 1921.
Now a ruin.

PORTLEMAN, Mullingar
Severe, three storey, late eighteenth-century house with Doric portico in antis. Good carved main staircase. Seat of the De Blaquieres at the end of the eighteenth century.
Demolished c.1941.

RATHCONNELL COURT, Mullingar
Late eighteenth-century Gothic house.   Now a ruin.

ROSMEAD, Delvin
Large, three storey, late eighteenth-century house. Seat of W.H. Wood in 1814. Now a ruin. Stone columns from the house were used in 1942 in the rebuilding of Balrath Burry, Co. Meath.

SHUROCK, Moate
Originally a small early eighteenth-century house, but much altered in the late eighteenth century and early nineteenth century.   Now a ruin.

SONNA, Ballynacarrigy
Three storey eighteenth-century house with flanking single storey wings. Seat of the Tuites.
Demolished.

TORR, Tyrrellspass
A late eighteenth-century house with bows at each end.
Now a ruin.

TUDENHAM PARK, Mullingar
A large three storey house of very high quality built c.1742 for George Rochfort and attributed to Richard Castle. Very fine interior which included a large entrance hall with screens of columns at both ends. Some reception rooms and the main staircase were altered c.1790 and had good neo-classical plasterwork. The house was stripped c.1957-58 and is now a ruin which should be preserved.

VIOLETSTOWN, Mullingar
Seat of F.P. Smyth in 1814.   Demolished.

WATERSTON, Athlone
Very fine three storey house designed by Richard Castle in the 1740's for Gustavus Handcock M.P. Interior with good plasterwork.   Now a ruin.

Left:
Baronstown: Entrance front.
Collection: Geoffrey Brooke.

Facing page:
Tudenham: Entrance front 1961.
Photograph: Hugh Doran.

Left to right:

Shurock: Doorcase c.1975.
Photograph: William Garner.

Gaybrook: Entrance front c.1975.
Photograph: William Garner.

Gaulstown: Entrance front.
Photograph: Maurice Craig.

Moydrum Castle: Entrance front c.1860.

Left to right:

Drumcree House: Main staircase in ruins 1968.
Photograph: David Davison.

Drumcree House: Entrance front 1968.
Photograph: David Davison.

Kildevin: Entrance front c.1975.
Photograph: William Garner.

Rosmead: Entrance front.
Photograph: Lord Rossmore.

Above:
Killua Castle: Entrance front.
Photograph: Gillman Collection.

Right:
Killua Castle: Garden front c.1970.
Photograph: Lord Rossmore.

Facing page:
Castleboro, Co. Wexford.
Photograph: Robert French, Lawrence Collection, Nat. Library of Ireland.

COUNTY WEXFORD

BALLYANNE HOUSE, New Ross
Late eighteenth-century house with good interior. The seat of General Ambrose in 1814.   Demolished.

BALLY ELLIS, Gorey
Two storey, early to mid eighteenth-century, gable-ended house with later single storey Doric portico.   Demolished.

BALLYNASTRAGH (eighteenth-century house), Gorey
A three storey mid eighteenth-century house built by Sir Thomas Esmonde incorporating some seventeenth-century work. The single storey Doric portico may date from the early nineteenth century. Battlements were added to the house later in the nineteenth century and further alterations were carried out to the design of George Ashlin. Burnt in 1923. A very attractive modern house designed by Dermot Gogarty was built in 1937.

CAMOLIN PARK, Camolin
An early to mid eighteenth-century house having a good segmental pedimented doorcase. The seat of the Annesleys, Earls of Mountnorris.   Demolished 1974.

CASTLEBORO, Enniscorthy
A superb classical house built *c.*1840 to the design of Daniel Robertson for 1st Lord Carew. Entrance front with very fine Corinthian portico in granite. Impressive interior with two storey entrance hall, imperial staircase and oval drawing-room.
The house was burnt in 1923. Now a ruin which must be preserved as it is one of the most magnificent ruins in the country.

COOLBAWN, Enniscorthy
A large Tudor Revival house built in the 1830's to the design of Frederick Darley for Francis Bruen. Burnt in 1914.
Now a ruin.

COURTOWN HOUSE, Gorey
Originally a three storey, early eighteenth-century, 'U' plan house. Damaged during the 1798 rebellion. Altered and enlarged 1865-1867 to the design of William Burn for the 5th Earl of Courtown.   Demolished after the Second World War.

Above:
Castleboro: Library c.1890.
Photograph: Robert French, Lawrence Coll., Nat. Library of Ireland.

Facing page:
Macmine Castle: Entrance front c.1900.
Collection: P.A. Crane. Copy photograph: David Davison.

MACMINE CASTLE, Enniscorthy

An early to mid nineteenth-century castle incorporating a tower house. The seat of the Richards family.   Now a ruin.

MOUNTFIN, Enniscorthy

A three storey early eighteenth-century house with projecting tower-like end bays.   Demolished.

OAKLANDS, New Ross

A two storey late Georgian house with single storey pedimented portico. In 1814 the seat of R. Jones Sankey. Destroyed by fire 1956.

SAINT EDANS, Ferns

Plain three storey house built *c.*1800, once the Palace of the Bishop of Ferns.   Now a ruin.

SAUNDERS COURT, Kyle

An early to mid eighteenth-century house with later alterations. The superb main entrance gates survive. In 1814 the seat of the Earl of Arran.   Demolished.

SOLSBOROUGH, Enniscorthy

Nineteenth-century house. Now a ruin. Very fine mid eighteenth-century gate-piers survive.

TOTTENHAM GREEN, Taghmon

An important, single storey, late seventeenth-century or early eighteenth-century, pedimented and gable-ended house. Built for the Tottenhams. Very fine pedimented Roman Ionic doorcase and steep roof with dormer-windows. The pediment had a Venetian window. A wing was added to the left hand side later in the eighteenth century.   Demolished *c.*1950.

TYKILLAN, Kyle
Three storey mid Georgian house with later single storey porch.
Demolished.

UPTON HOUSE, Kilmuckridge
A two storey late eighteenth-century house with early to mid
nineteenth-century porch and wide eaved roof. In 1814 the seat
of William Moreton.   Burnt in 1923.

WILTON CASTLE, Enniscorthy
Very fine early nineteenth-century castle designed by Daniel
Robertson for the Alcocks, replacing an early eighteenth-century
house, the doorcase of which survives in the stable yard. Burnt
in 1923.   Now a spectacular ruin.

Below:
Coolbawn.
Old photograph. Print: Richard Dann.

Facing, top:
Tykillan.
Old photograph. Copy photograph: David Davison.

Facing, bottom:
Wilton Castle: Old postcard view.
Gillman Collection.

Powerscourt: Saloon c.1970.
Photograph: William Ryan.

COUNTY WICKLOW

BALLARDEBEG, Ashford
Demolished. Stables remain.

BELLVUE, Delgany
A two storey house built *c.*1754 for David La Touche. Altered and enlarged *c.*1790 to the design of Whitmore Davis and again in the early nineteenth century when Richard Morrison added a chapel.   Demolished in the 1950's.

BLESSINGTON HOUSE, Blessington
Very fine, late seventeenth-century, 'H' plan house. Entrance front with colonnade between projecting wings. Built for Michael Boyle, Archbishop of Armagh, and Lord Chancellor of Ireland. Burnt in 1798.

GLENCORMAC, Bray
Very fine, late nineteenth-century, brick, two storey house. Good interior with imperial staircase. Destroyed by fire.   Demolished.

GLENDALOUGH HOUSE, Annamoe
Large Tudor Revival house possibly designed by Daniel Robertson *c.*1838 incorporating an earlier house to the rere built for Thomas Barton. Additions were made in the late nineteenth century.   The main part of the house was demolished *c.*1977.

HILLBROOK, Carnew
Very attractive early eighteenth-century house with a simple lugged doorcase. The roof was altered in the late nineteenth century. The former home of the Symes family.   Demolished.

KILMACURRAGH, Rathdrum
Very important late seventeenth-century house built in 1697 for Thomas Acton. Possibly designed by Sir William Robinson, surveyor general. The five bay pedimented entrance front retained its original baroque wooden doorcase (unique in Ireland) and high-pitched roof. The entire interior was panelled and had a very fine carved staircase. Single storey wings were added in the 1840's but otherwise the house remained almost unaltered. Empty for about twenty years. The roof was badly damaged by fire in 1978. The house is now little more than a ruin.

POWERSCOURT, Enniskerry
Outstanding Palladian house designed by Richard Castle for Richard Wingfield M.P. and built 1731-1740, but incorporating the remains of an earlier castle. The garden front was refaced and an extra storey added in the 1770's. The house was much altered and added to in the nineteenth century, to the designs of Daniel Robertson and William Burn. Some of Richard Castle's interiors survived including the entrance hall with its stucco shell decoration, the main staircase and most important of all the saloon on the first floor, 60'x 40' and 40' high, an adaptation of a Vitruvian 'Egyptian Hall', and also the cedar room on the garden front. The house was sold to Mr. & Mrs. Ralph Slazenger who also bought the contents. The restoration of the house was completed the day before the house was destroyed by fire in November 1974 along with most of its contents. The destruction of Powerscourt was the greatest single loss to Irish country house architecture since the civil war. The central block of the house is now a ruin.

RATH HOUSE, Tullow
Strange, two storey, granite faced, early nineteenth-century house. Pediment over entire front and entrance via Greek Doric porch in 'antis. Good elliptical top-lit stair hall. This house incorporates an early eighteenth-century house at the rere. Derelict.

ROSSANAGH, Ashford
An important, early eighteenth-century, three storey, brick house built and altered for the Tighe family. While this house has not been demolished, the wings, one of which contained the superb saloon, have been; this room was one of the most important panelled rooms in Ireland. It was offered for sale on the London art market in 1929, and is now said to be in the U.S.A.

SAUNDERS GROVE, Baltinglass
A very fine, large, early eighteenth-century house built in 1716 for Morley Saunders. The entrance front had a pedimented breakfront and a superb granite rusticated Doric doorcase added *c.*1740. The garden front was of brick and with cut stone dressing. The house was destroyed by fire in 1923 and a new house was built on the same site in 1925 incorporating the original front doorcase and area railings.

STRATFORD LODGE, Baltinglass
A three storey late eighteenth-century house built for the Earl of Aldborough; linked to single storey pavilions by straight screen walls.   Demolished.

TINNEHINCH, Enniskerry
A large eighteenth-century house formerly an inn of three storeys with a five bay recessed centre which had a single bay pedimented breakfront, flanked by single bay wings (possibly later additions) of only two floors but of the same overall height. Seat of Henry Grattan. The house has been demolished except for the ground floor front wall of the entrance front which now forms an attractive garden feature.

TOBER, Dunlavin
A three storey, five bay, early eighteenth-century house. Now a ruin.

Powerscourt:
The Cedar Room c.1965.
Photograph: Lord Rossmore.

Above:
Rossanagh: Saloon chimneypiece c.1929.
Copy photograph: David Davison.

Top right:
Saunders Grove: Garden front from the cascade c.1890.
Photograph: Robert French, Lawrence Studio, Dublin.
Copy photograph: David Davison.

Centre right:
Glendalough House.
Old photograph. Collection: Mr. R.A. Childers.

Bottom right:
Kilmacurragh: Entrance front 1978.
Photograph: David Davison.

Index

Authorities

An Taisce and the Irish Historic Properties Reports: *Heritage at Risk*, Dublin 1977. *Safeguarding Historic Houses*, Dublin 1985. J. Begley *The diocese of Limerick from 1691 to the present time*, Dublin 1938. Mark Bence-Jones *Twilight of the Ascendancy*, London 1987. John Betjeman *High and Low*, London 1966. Elizabeth Bowen *Bowenscourt and Seven Winters*, London 1984. Eyre Crowe *Today in Ireland*, London 1825. Christina Edgeworth Colvin *Maria Edgeworth's Tours of Ireland. III: Connaught Studia Neophilologica*, Vol.XLIII No.2 1971. Arthur Irwin Dasent *John Thadeus Delane . . . his life and Correspondence*, London 1908. Frank Delaney *Betjeman Country*, London 1983. Thomas Flanagan *The Irish Novelists*, New York 1959. Constantine FitzGibbon *Miss Finnigan's Fault*, London 1953. Elizabeth, Countess of Fingall *Seventy Years Young*, London 1937. Sean Feehan *The Magic of Shannon*, Cork 1980. Oliver St. John Gogarty *Rolling down the Lea*, London 1950. Gerald Griffin *The Rivals* and *Tracy's Ambition*, London 1830. Richard Gill *Happy Rural Seat, the English Country House and the Literary Imagination* (Particularly for Yeats and Bowen), Newhaven and London 1972. J. Anthony Gaughan *The Knights of Glin*, Dublin 1978. John B. Keane 'Interview with Deirdre Purcell' *Sunday Tribune* 28 Feb. 1988. Gertrude Lyster (editor) *A Family Chronicle, notes and letter selected by Barbarina, the Hon. Lady Gray*, London 1908. Hermoine Lee (editor) *The Mulberry Tree, Writings of Elizabeth Bowen* (includes 'The Big House' 1946), London 1986. Charles Macklin *The True Born Irishman*, Dublin 1783. Lewis Mac Neice *The Poetry of W.B. Yeats*, London 1970. Gordon St. George Mark, 'Tyrone House' *Irish Georgian Society Bulletin*, July-Dec. 1976. James Matthews *Voices, a life of Frank O'Connor*, Dublin 1983. Constantina Maxwell *Country and Town in Ireland under the Georges*, Dundalk 1949. Sir Herbert Maxwell Bart (editor) *The Creevy Papers*, London 1904 and John Gore (editor) *Creevy's Life and Times*, London. J.P. Mayer (editor), Alexis de Tocqueville *Journeys to England and Ireland*, Yale 1958. Patrick Melvin, 'The Composition of the Galway Gentry' *The Irish Genealogist*, Vol.7 1986. Hugh Montgomery Massingberd 'Folly in a troubled land' *Sunday Telegraph* Oct. 17 1987. George Moore *A Story-Teller's Holiday*, London 1928. George Moore *Hail and Farewell Ave*, London 1947. Kevin Myers 'An Irishman's Diary' *The Irish Times* Sept 4. 1986. Frank O'Connor *Irish Miles*, London. Frank O'Connor *Leinster, Munster and Connaught*, London 1949. Nuala O'Faolain 'Preserving our past for our future' *The Irish Times* May 23 1988. Prince von Pückler Muskau *Tour in England, Ireland and France*, London 1832. Desmond Roche 'The Later Clanricardes' *Clanricarde Country*, Galway 1987. C.J. Woods 'Johann Friedrich Herings description of Connaught, 1806-7' *Irish Historical Studies* XXV No.99 (May 1987). Nigel Nicholson and J. Troutmann (Editors) *The Sickle Side of the Moon* Virginia Woolf, letters 1932-1935. London 1982. W.B. Yeats *Collected Poems*, London 1955. Margaret Ferrier Young (editor) *The Letters of a Noble Woman* (Mrs. La Touche of Harristown), London 1908.